Family Circles

A comedy

Alan Ayckbourn

Samuel French — London
New York - Toronto - Hollywood

FAMILY CIRCLES

This play has had several incarnations, starting life at the Library Theatre, Scarborough on 20th August, 1970 as *The Story So Far...*

It was re-written and re-titled a number of times, touring at one point with Celia Johnson as Emma before culminating in this final version which was first produced at the Orange Tree Theatre, Richmond on 24th November, 1978 with the following cast:

Edward	Rio Fanning
Emma	Jan Bashford
Jenny	Jan Carey
Deirdre	Liz Crowther
James	David Gillies
Oliver	Michael Wynne
David	Brian Miller
Polly	Auriol Smith

Directed by Sam Walters

CHARACTERS

Edward Gray
Emma Gray
Polly
Jenny } their daughters
Deirdre
Oliver
David } their daughters' men
James

The action of the play takes place in the living-room of the Grays' house

Time: an August weekend

PRODUCTION NOTE

During the first three scenes of the play, everyone, with
the exception of Edward and Emma, takes on a different
relative role; that is, they remain the same person, but have
a different partner in each scene.

In the last scene (Act II, Scene 2), everyone, again with the
exception of Edward and Emma, appears in the various
roles they played in the previous three scenes, so they are
numbered according to the scene in which their character
role first appeared. Thus, the Deirdre who enters at the
start of this scene is known as Deirdre 1—the one that first
arrived with James 1, and so on.

SYNOPSIS OF SCENES

ACT I

SCENE 1   *Saturday Afternoon*
Polly and David
Jenny and Oliver
Deirdre and James

SCENE 2   *Saturday Afternoon, later*
Polly and James
Jenny and David
Deirdre and Oliver

ACT II

SCENE 1   *Saturday Night*
Polly and Oliver
Jenny and James
Deirdre and David

SCENE 2   *Sunday Morning*
All

Plays by Alan Ayckbourn published by Samuel French Ltd

Absent Friends
Absurd Person Singular
Bedroom Farce
Callisto 5
A Chorus of Disapproval
Communicating Doors
Confusions
A Cut in the Rates
Dreams from a Summer House
Ernie's Incredible Illucinations
Henceforward ...
How the Other Half Loves
Intimate Exchanges (Volume 1)
Intimate Exchanges (Volume 2)
Joking Apart
Just Between Ourselves
Living Together
Man of the Moment
Mixed Doubles (*with other authors*)
Mr A's Amazing Maze Plays
Mr Whatnot
My Very Own Story
The Norman Conquests
Relatively Speaking
The Revengers' Comedies
Round and Round the Garden
Season's Greetings
Sisterly Feelings
A Small Family Business
Suburban Strains
Table Manners
Taking Steps
Ten Times Table
This Is Where We Came In
Time and Time Again
Time of My Life
Tons of Money (*revisor*)
Way Upstream
Wildest Dreams
Wolf at the Door (*adaptor*)
Woman in Mind

ACT I

SCENE 1

The Grays' living-room. Comfortably middle class

There are several doors off; one to the kitchen; one to the hall and front door; french windows leading to the garden. A staircase leads via a landing balcony to the upstairs rooms

Emma, a pleasant if rather fraught woman in her mid-fifties, is busy laying a table-cloth on a tea table

After a few moments, Edward, her husband, aged about sixty, enters. He has returned from his walk, hatted and wielding a stout stick

Edward (*seeing Emma*) Hah!
Emma (*without looking up*) Good walk, dear? Worked up a good appetite? Tea won't be very long.

Edward looks out of the window

Thinking of mowing the lawn? It does need it, I agree. I've made some Mummy's Delights. You know, those little cakes of mine. The ones the girls love. You seemed to like them, too, I remember. That's Oliver's new car in the drive. Have you seen it? Enormous. Well, I suppose they need it. With their family. He's in the garden somewhere. Did you see him? And Jenny's busy buttering bread for me. Isn't that kind? She's been telling me they seem to be getting on a little better. That's good news, isn't it?
Edward Who are?
Emma Jenny and Oliver, dear. They seem to have worked out one or two of their little problems.
Edward Disastrous.
Emma Mmm? What's that, dear?
Edward Of all the men Jenny had to choose, not that she had any choice when it came down to it, I don't know why she chose him.
Emma Oliver's doing very well for himself...
Edward Exactly. Far too clever for her. She's as thick as a Portuguese gangplank.

Emma That's not a very nice thing to say about your daughter, is it?
Edward Oh, she's a *nice* girl. Very *nice*. But I don't know... Only one
absolutely certain thing you can say about marriage. Whoever you decide
on to share your life with invariably turns out to be the worst possible
choice you could have made, present company excepted, of course. Fact
of life.
Emma There are those who say that Oliver is a little stuffy for her.
Edward Stuffy?
Emma She's a very considerate girl, anyway.
Edward Born worrier like her mother, that's all. Think I'll go and have a
word with Oliver. Show him my dahlias.
Emma Oh, yes. Do that.
Edward Stuffy or not, he certainly appreciates my dahlias. More than can
be said for some of them.

*Jenny, a woman of twenty-eight, enters carrying two plates of sandwiches.
She is obviously pregnant*

Jenny Hallo, Father. How are you?
Edward Hallo, Jenny.
Jenny (*kissing him awkwardly on the cheek*) Many, many, congratulations.
Edward Mmm?
Jenny Congratulations.
Emma She means our anniversary, Father.
Edward Oh, yes. Yes, thank you. And to you. I'm just going to go and sort
out your husband. Show him how to grow dahlias. Not like the forget-me-
nots he grows. No business calling them dahlias at all...

Edward goes out

Jenny (*calling after him*) See you later. (*To Emma*) Mother, I don't know
if you got enough butter. We seem to be running awfully short.
Emma (*concentrating*) Now, there may possibly be some more in the bread
bin.
Jenny The bread bin?
Emma Yes, I seem to remember putting some in there. I don't know why
I did now. I seem to remember I had a very good reason at the time... Yes,
I remember. It was to remind me, when I got the bread out, to remember
to buy some more butter.
Jenny (*patiently*) Yes, Mother. If you'd only make a list...
Emma Oh, darling, you know me. The first thing I do is lose it.
Jenny Oliver and I bought you that little silver note pad for your birthday,
specially.

Emma So you did. I must try and use that. That's a good idea. I wonder where I put it.
Jenny Mother, honestly...

Deirdre, a girl of twenty-four, enters noisily. She is followed at a discreet distance by James, a rather lost-looking young man in his mid-twenties, laden with her luggage. He is dressed rather incongruously in white shorts

Deirdre Nobody move. Don't panic. We've arrived.
Emma (*with great joy*) Deirdre...
Deirdre Hallo, Ma.
Emma (*hugging her*) How nice. This is nice. You know, I wondered for a moment if you'd remember... (*She sees James*) Oh...
Deirdre Oh. Dump it down there, Jas. Ma, this is Jas.
Emma Jas?
Jenny (*staring at the luggage; to Deirdre*) How long have you come for?
James How do you do, Mrs Gray? (*He shakes hands with difficulty*)
Emma Yes, how do you do. (*To Deirdre*) Jas, did you say, dear?

James unloads the luggage in the hall

Deirdre James. I call him Jas. James is a boring name. Almost as boring as Deirdre.
Emma (*a little taken aback*) Oh. Well. That's nice. We have an extra for tea then, Jenny.
Jenny And presumably for dinner.
Deirdre Dinner?
Jenny We're going out to dinner tonight. I told you in my letter.
Deirdre Oh God, so you did.
Jenny Oliver and I booked the table.
Emma Well, that's all right. If Deirdre wants to bring her young man along, it'll make it even jollier. Why not? It just means eight instead of seven. That's easily arranged, surely?
Jenny (*fiercely; to Deirdre*) I mean, all you had to do was to phone me or drop me a card telling me you were bringing someone.
Deirdre I didn't know I was when you wrote. I only met Jas on Thursday, didn't I, Jas?
James Yes. I'm sorry if I...
Jenny Yes, well, I'm sorry too. I don't want you to feel unwelcome. (*As she goes to the kitchen*) It's just that it does make things terribly difficult when people spring things on you like this at the very last minute.

Jenny has gone

Deirdre She hasn't changed, has she?

Emma You must understand, dear, she's a lot of things worrying her at the moment.

Deirdre What's wrong? Has Ollie been shouting at her again?

Emma I don't know, dear. Presumably with the baby on the way and—well, I never ask about these things. You know me, so long as all of you are happy, I don't enquire. Now do sit down—Jas—and feel very welcome.

James (*still uneasy*) Thank you. I'm very sorry, I don't really seem to have come dressed for the occasion. I'm sorry. Perhaps I'd——

Emma Of course not. Deirdre's sister is a little bit excitable——

Deirdre Ha!

Emma —But she does mean well. If you'll excuse me a moment, I must get on with the tea.

James Of course.

Deirdre How's Pa then?

Emma Oh, much the same, dear, much the same.

Emma goes out to the kitchen

Deirdre (*half to herself*) Sorry to hear that. (*To James*) Well, this is it. Home. Does this explain to you why I wake up in the middle of the night screaming?

James You didn't tell me this was going to be a big family thing. I can't go out to dinner dressed like this.

Deirdre You look fantastic.

James I thought this was just to be a quiet weekend.

Deirdre No, well, it's Ma and Pa's anniversary, you see. We usually all come down for that. Particularly if they're at weekends and in this case it's—Oh, God!

James What is it?

Deirdre I never got them anything. Hell! I meant to buy them something at the station. Chocolates or crisps or something. I forgot all about it.

James Oh. We could always nip back to that village and——

Deirdre No. Don't bother. They'll get plenty. Jenny will have bought something. Embroidered oven mitts with "I love Mother" on them, no doubt. And Polly will probably bring them a loaded shotgun... In all the excitement they'll never notice.

James (*worried*) Should have got them something, though. I mean it's the thought...

Deirdre Oh, don't be so boring. I barely like them—either of them—I'm certainly not going to be a hypocrite as well. Look, can you amuse yourself for a minute? I'd better go and jolly up sister cow-face in the kitchen. Break it to Mother you're staying the night.

James Don't you think it would be better if I went back earlier? (*He indicates his attire*) I mean I'm hardly——
Deirdre No, I damn well don't. I need you here. You might help to keep me sane. Why do you think I brought you? There's the spare room going free. It's full of horn gramophones and Father's old dress uniforms, but it's still habitable. It's also next to mine. Wink, wink. Won't be a sec. Amuse yourself. Kick the furniture or something.

Deirdre goes out

James prowls about

After a while, Oliver, a man still in his thirties but whose manner suggests he can't wait to get into his fifties, enters. He stares at James without speaking

James (*at length*) Hallo.
Oliver Hallo. Oliver.
James James.
Oliver Hallo.
James Hi.

A pause

I'm with Deirdre. A friend of Deirdre's.
Oliver Are you? (*He nods*)
James (*trying again*) Got a terrific view from your window here.
Oliver Yes, indeed. (*He moves to the table*) Absolutely first class. Would you say these were tuna fish?
James Sorry?
Oliver They smell like tuna fish. Hope to God they are. The alternative's too terrible to contemplate. (*He laughs*)
James (*joining in uncertainly*) Yes.
Oliver Been having a look at Edward's dahlias. Got to hand it to him. They're good, very good. Mind you, he's a specialist. He can't grow anything else. His lawn's in a terrible state. Seen the lawn?
James I think I—walked over it.
Oliver Terrible state. Dandelions. Well, you've chosen a good weekend you have.
James So I understand. Deirdre didn't actually tell me that——
Oliver You'll probably live to regret it. You know these family do's. Especially this family. Get a bit out of hand. Not so much a beargarden, more a... (*He tails off and gazes into the distance, clicking his fingers thoughtfully—a habit he has*)

James (*after a pause*) Yes.
Oliver Anyway.
James Yes.
Oliver I say, did you know you had shorts on?
James Yes.
Oliver Yes. It is fairly humid, I suppose. Ninety-three for four at lunch.
James Ah.
Oliver Not bad that. Ninety-three for four. Another couple of quick wickets... Drive down, did you?
James No, train. With Deirdre.
Oliver Oh, yes. You know, I'm not at all sure these are tuna fish. (*He investigates*) I'm married to her sister, you know. That's her sister Jenny. Met her, have you, my wife?
James Yes, just now.
Oliver She's all right. Speak slowly to her or she misses the point.
James (*smiling uncertainly*) Oh...

Deirdre enters hurriedly. She is clutching the fastening of her trousers with one hand

Deirdre (*yelling behind her*) Where? (*To James and Oliver*) Excuse me, folks.
James Hallo.
Deirdre (*going back to the door*) Where, Ma?
Emma (*off*) In the top drawer.
Deirdre (*to James*) All right, love? Oh, hallo, Ollie. God, you're not stuck with Ollie, are you? That's a fate worse than Father.
James No, we've just been——
Deirdre (*yelling*) Top drawer, did you say?
Emma (*off*) Yes, dear. In the tin. The little blue tin.
Deirdre (*to James*) Safety pin. Bust my zip.
James Oh. No, Oliver was just——
Deirdre (*searching in a drawer*) Little blue tin... Mother has little red tins, little green tins and little blue tins all over the house. And only Mother knows what's in them. (*She finds what she's looking for*) Ah. Right. Operation Emergency Pins. Won't be a sec. (*Yelling*) Got them.

Deirdre goes out

Oliver Well, I take my hat off to you, coping with her.
James Great fun.
Oliver So's a broken neck, I understand. In business, are you?
James No. Pleasure, really. (*He smiles at his joke*)
Oliver Don't quite follow you.

James I always say that. When people say, "Are you in business?", I always say, "No, pleasure".

Oliver Do you?

James I sell sports equipment, you see.

Oliver Sports equipment, eh? (*He looks thoughtful*)

James That's how I met Deirdre, actually.

Oliver Football boots, you mean? That sort of thing?

James That sort of thing, yes. She came in to buy a squash racquet and I sold her one.

Oliver Deirdre plays squash?

James That's the point, no.

Oliver No?

James She wanted to learn. I offered to teach her. Last night.

Oliver Mmmm?

James Squash.

Oliver Ah.

James But when I came round to collect her, she found she hadn't any suitable shoes. So we went to the cinema instead.

Oliver Ah.

James Just as well, really. I've never played squash in my life.

Oliver No?

James First time I've ever been to a film in tennis shorts, though.

Oliver What would be your biggest selling line, then?

James At the shop? Footballs, I suppose ... and—gentlemen's supports... (*He gestures*) About fifty-fifty, really.

Oliver (*watching him intently*) Is that size or quantity?

James Quantity.

Oliver Mmm, surprising. A conclusion to be drawn somewhere there I should imagine. I might have a pair in the boot.

James I beg your pardon?

Oliver Trousers. If you feel the need for trousers.

James Oh, yes, thank you.

Oliver moves to the table again

Oliver They look like blackcurrant jam.

James Oh, I don't mind what colour they are.

Oliver (*irritated; indicating sandwiches*) No, no, no.

Jenny comes in with more plates of food. She looks hot, flustered and a little tired

Jenny Have Polly and David arrived yet?

Oliver Not yet.

Jenny Well, it's really too bad. Mother's all on her own out there. There's only me helping. Deirdre's split her trousers or something. She cut one slice of bread, ruined the loaf and split her trousers. I understand you're staying with us, Mr...?

James If it's no trouble.

Jenny Not at all. It's no trouble for me. I'm sure Deirdre will arrange everything, make sure you're comfortable.

James (*indicating his shorts*) I was wondering if I——

Jenny (*to Oliver*) I've told Mother we must leave here by seven, Oliver. They won't hold that table reservation if we're late.

Oliver Bags of time. If we leave at... (*He trails off, fingers clicking*)

Jenny (*gently*) Don't do that, dear.

Oliver What?

Jenny That—clicking. You keep doing it lately.

Oliver Why shouldn't I?

Jenny Because it's just a little bit irritating, dear.

Oliver gives her a look

I'll phone Mrs Curtis after tea and make sure the children aren't playing up.

Oliver I should forget them. Out of sight, out of mind.

Jenny Yes, I know, dear. But somebody has to worry about them, don't they?

Oliver Don't see why. They never worry about us.

Jenny Honestly, it's too bad. I'm the only one out there helping, Oliver, the only one. There's masses to do. (*More confidentially*) Oh ... and there's been some trouble.

Oliver Trouble?

Jenny Yes, Mother's hinted at it. I mean, she said nothing definite but I could read between the lines. And I didn't tell you, I also... (*She counts side plates*) Two, four, five...

James Er...

Oliver Are those tuna fish, do you happen to know?

Jenny Crab, I think. No, I didn't tell you I had a... Oh no, you don't like crab, do you?

Oliver I had rather hoped I'd got that point to register by now. Still...

Jenny I'll see if there's anything else. There's some cheese spread, I think.

Oliver It's all right, don't panic. I just won't eat them, will I?

Jenny Are you sure?

Oliver Quite sure. I'll stick to the blackcurrant jam.

Jenny (*no less alarmed*) It's home-made damson.

Oliver Fine, fine, fine.

Deirdre enters

Deirdre There we are. I'm decent again. You'll have to bury me in these trousers now. I'll never get them off again. But I am decent. And decency is all, around here.

Jenny Deirdre, do come and help. Mother's doing it all.

Deirdre Mother always does it all. She likes doing it all. It's so she can droop finally at the tea table, pale and exhausted, amidst scattered applause.

Jenny That's beside the point. It's supposed to be a party for her.

Deirdre Thirty-two glorious years...

Oliver Celebrated with crab sandwiches. Very fitting.

Deirdre Crab? Super.

Jenny You really are the laziest little devil. Well, you can do the plates, then. I've got a terrible headache coming, I can feel it.

Jenny goes out to the kitchen

James Look, I——

Deirdre Hallo, Jas, darling. Are you terribly bored?

James No...

Deirdre Oliver, have you been boring Jas?

Oliver (*picking up a newspaper*) I've hardly said a word. (*He makes for the hall*)

Deirdre Exactly. You get the same sensation talking to Oliver as you do yelling into an old laundry bag.

Oliver (*at the hall door*) Very dangerous all this luggage here. Nearly fell over it just now.

Deirdre That is all I have in the world.

Oliver Oh, it's yours, is it? I take it you like to travel prepared?

Deirdre I am in the process of changing residence, actually.

Oliver Oh, got somewhere nicer?

Deirdre Not quite. I had rather sudden notice to quit, that's all.

Oliver When was this?

Deirdre Last night. My landlord objected to the use of the bath...

Oliver Seems a bit unreasonable.

Deirdre That's just what Jas and I felt. We sat there and argued with him till the water turned cold.

Deirdre wanders to the tea table. James smiles sheepishly at Oliver

Oh, God, she's made some of those awful cakes. Mummy's Delights. (*To James*) Whatever you do, steer clear of these. They're foul.

Oliver I wouldn't say that to her face. I seem to remember she's rather proud of them. (*He sits with the paper*)

Deirdre She always comes up with these. The first time she made them, we

all three took one bite... And when Mother was out of the room, Polly
tipped the whole plateful into a paper bag and hid it under the sofa. Mother
comes back in and she says "What's this? All gone?" she says, "I must
make some more of those." And for ever after... I can't remember how we
got rid of them eventually. Oh yes, used them as ammunition against the
boy next door, that's right. Made super ammo. Polly hit him right between
the eyes with one. Stopped him peeing through our fence, anyway. Filthy
little beast. By the way, have they arrived yet?
Oliver Who?
Deirdre Polly and David?
Oliver No.
Deirdre With any luck they won't come.
James Why?
Deirdre Oh, just you wait. David twitches. And when he's not twitching he's
fussing. And Polly's never really happy unless she's having a row with
someone, especially Father.
James (*smiling feebly*) Sounds fun.
Oliver (*without looking up from his paper*) Been some trouble, apparently.
Deirdre What?
Oliver Jen was saying so. She's probably got it wrong, mind you. Trouble.
With Mother and Father.
Deirdre Let's hear something new.

Jenny enters, agitated

Jenny Mother's cut herself on the pickles.
Oliver She's what?
Jenny (*tensely*) Mother has cut herself on the pickles and I don't think I can
cope. Oliver ... please, quickly... I think I'm going to faint.
Oliver (*used to this*) Now don't be silly, Jenny, sit down. Sit down. Head
between your knees... (*He steers her to a chair*)
Deirdre Elastoplast. (*She opens a drawer*) Wonder what colour tin she keeps
that in... (*She searches*)

Oliver rams Jenny's head between her knees

Jenny (*muffled*) Oh, my God.
Oliver (*calmly*) You must stop making everything into a crisis, Jenny. You'll
have nothing in reserve when World War Three breaks out.
Jenny Please, Oliver, do something. She is bleeding out there.
Deirdre Can't find the Elastoplast.
Oliver (*wearily*) It's in the kitchen dresser, if I remember correctly. I'll deal
with it, don't worry. I've dealt with it before.

Oliver goes out

Deirdre How did she manage to cut herself on a pickle? That's pretty good going, even for Mother.
Jenny (*through gritted teeth*) She was trying to open the pickle jar. I told her to leave it to me. Her hand slipped and she cut herself on the lid.
Deirdre (*jubilant*) Isn't that typical?
Jenny For God's sake, Deirdre, she's bleeding all over the bread board out there.

Jenny rushes out

Deirdre That's this house for you. Instant panic. If the lavatory doesn't flush properly they call out the fire brigade.
James Do you think your mother's all right?
Deirdre A teeny cut, I bet you. But Mother has the sort of manner that instils instant lack of confidence. She is entirely responsible for this whole twitching family.
James (*anxiously*) You don't twitch, do you?
Deirdre Not me. I swung the other way. The whole house could fall down for all I'd care.
James With them in it?
Deirdre Preferably. Are you shocked?
James (*uncertainly*) No. I was just thinking how people change as soon as they get home with their families.
Deirdre I suspect you're one of those unfashionable people with a happy childhood.
James Yes, I suppose it was really, I——

Oliver comes back from the kitchen

Deirdre Right. (*To James*) Conducted tours time.
James What?
Deirdre Round the estate, along the privets, twice round the rhubarb and back for tea.
James But, Deirdre, I must get hold of a pair of trousers.
Deirdre Excuse us.
Oliver Of course.

Jenny enters

Jenny Where are you going now?
Deirdre Out.

Deirdre and James go out the front door

Jenny She hasn't done these plates now.
Oliver (*in his newspaper again*) Plates?
Jenny They need napkins putting on them all, then they're ready to hand out.
Oliver Good idea.
Jenny (*starting on the plates*) I've got a splitting headache.
Oliver I should take something for it, then.
Jenny Oliver, you really should have a word with Mother.
Oliver Mmm?
Jenny We're the only ones she can turn to, you know.
Oliver What's that?
Jenny The point is, I phoned Polly this morning just to check she'd remember to bring some spare sheets—and she told me—well, she didn't go into detail but—I pray God it won't—but—we may have to try and get Father certified.
Oliver (*looking up*) Get him what?
Jenny (*agitated*) It may come to it. God, it may come to that.
Oliver (*sharply*) Jenny, will you please sit there, put your head back between your knees again and bloody well simmer down.
Jenny I didn't want to tell you before, in case it upset you.
Oliver (*angrily*) Upset me? Upset me, did you say?

Emma enters from the kitchen with more plates

Emma Oh, Oliver. Where's Father? I thought he was with you?
Oliver I left him beating the butterflies off his dahlias with his hat and bellowing at old Cartwright from next door.
Emma (*surveying the table*) Oh, dear. Do you think we've made enough?
Jenny Plenty, Mother. You've done plenty.
Emma We've a long drive ahead of us. I mean——
Oliver How's the hand?
Emma Oh, I can hardly feel it. Hardly at all.
Jenny If you'd asked me to open them in the first place——
Emma It's all right. Don't fuss, dear.
Jenny Well, sit down, Mother, just for a minute, please.
Emma Yes, I think I've earned it. Just for a second. (*She sits at the table*) Look, Oliver. We're using my new little spoons, see?
Oliver Oh, yes, they're nice. Who gave you those?
Jenny We did.
Emma Polly and David not arrived yet?
Oliver Not yet. They will no doubt do something appropriate like walk into the room when they do.

Emma (*concerned*) Oh, dear. You don't think anything can have——
Oliver With David driving at fifteen miles an hour along the grass verges it's unlikely, Mother.
Jenny It's unlikely, Mother.
Emma That dreadful old car of theirs. It's never safe. I sometimes wake up in the night, Jenny, and think... (*She sighs*) I dread to think what I think.
Oliver Mother, could I possibly remind you again that I don't care for crab.
Emma Now. I want you all to be very, very tactful this evening. For my sake.
Jenny I always am.
Oliver Anything but crab.
Emma You know, I sometimes think that Polly deliberately tries to annoy Father. And when Deirdre gets that naughty look in her eye... I can't think why, after all these years, you children haven't learnt that the only way to deal with Father is to ignore him.
Jenny From what I've heard that isn't enough.
Emma What do you mean, dear? From what you've heard?
Jenny (*darkly*) I've heard. Leave it at that.
Oliver I shouldn't try to follow it up, Mother. She's trying to tell us something. But it'll take a little time, as usual.
Emma All I'm saying, is, try and be tactful. You only have to see your Father about once a year.
Jenny What are you talking about? There's hardly a weekend Oliver and I aren't down here with the children.
Emma Yes, I know *you* are, dear.
Jenny (*flaring up*) Then tell Polly and Deirdre. I don't need lectures on being tactful. When I think of the times...
Oliver Jenny.
Jenny No, well, it's too bad. I mean, who went to all the trouble to arrange this evening? We did. Not Deirdre and Polly. They haven't done a stroke, either of them. Not a thing. I've been out there all afternoon, you know, Oliver, cutting cakes, icing sandwiches...
Oliver Jenny, quieten down.
Emma And do stop being so touchy, dear. She really is dreadfully touchy, don't you find that, Oliver? Even as a child she was always the one that whined.
Jenny Me, whine? That was Deirdre. Deirdre whined.
Emma That's not true, Jenny. Deirdre had a lovely nature. Everyone adored her. She had the sweetest little blue pinafore dress, Oliver, and little red socks.
Jenny Deirdre was always bawling her head off. I want, I want, that was her.
Emma If she did that, it was only because you two were so mean to her. Do you know, Oliver, what these two little beasts did to Deirdre one day in the park?

Jenny (*rising*) Oh, well, if you're going to drag that up again...
Emma I'd only left them alone for a second.
Jenny I'm not listening to this again.

Jenny goes out

Emma "Polly, Jenny," I said, "take good care of little Deirdre, Mummy's just going to spend a penny." And do you know what they did? They took Deirdre's dolly that she absolutely adored, tied a stone to its feet and threw it in the pond.
Oliver (*bored*) Too much television.
Emma Well. When I came back... "Mummy, mummy," she said, "they downed Diddy's dolly." She kept saying it over and over, utterly heartbroken. "They've downed Diddy's dolly." All the way home. Well. Those two had no supper that night, I can tell you. If I'd been their father I'd have spanked them but he was never... They really were difficult children. Do you find Jenny quite so difficult, Oliver?
Oliver Well, I don't let her get on top of me more than I can help. If you know what I mean. The way I look at it, as Father's very fond of saying—we all marry the wrong people. Not much you can do about it really. I remember when I went to ask Edward if he'd mind if I took one of his daughters off his hands, he said "Well, you've got a choice of three evils. If you marry Polly, you'll never get off the ground. If you marry Deirdre, you'll never come out of the clouds. And if you choose Jenny, you'll finish up somewhere between the two." Halfway up the wall, presumably. Too late to do a swap, isn't it? Leave her alone as much as I can. That's my philosophy.
Emma Well, I'm grateful she married you, Oliver. You're such a sensible person.

Jenny enters

Jenny (*grimly*) Polly and David have just arrived.
Emma Oh, thank goodness.
Oliver There's no need to look so tragic about it.
Emma (*going*) I'll put the kettle on.
Jenny Polly's got a face like thunder.
Emma Oh, dear.
Oliver Her normal expression, isn't it?

Emma goes out

Jenny Oliver.

Oliver Mmmm?
Jenny Have you said anything yet—about the trouble?
Oliver What trouble?
Jenny With Father. I left you alone just now, especially. So you could.
Oliver Ah. Is that why you left us alone. I wish you'd leave me alone. Go away.
Jenny You must talk to Mother. You're the only one of us who...

David enters. Early thirties, frenzied and fussy

David My God. Oh, my God, what a journey. Hallo, Ollie, Jenny. I must sit down. I must. *(He sits)*
Jenny Hallo, David. Tea won't be long. I'll just give Mother a hand.
David *(getting up again)* Jenny, love, I wonder if you could bring me a glass of water. I'm shaking. I'm literally trembling all over. *(He fumbles in his pocket for a bottle of pills)*
Jenny You poor thing.
David I'll have to take a couple of these.
Jenny Right, sit there. Try to calm down. Take deep breaths. I won't be a minute.

Jenny hurries out

David You don't know how lucky you are to be married to a nurse.
Oliver An ex-nurse.
David Never mind. She still has a training.
Oliver Not much of one. I understand she was off sick most of the time.
David Polly is being impossible. You've no idea, Oliver, absolutely impossible. She refused point blank to let me drive down here. I don't know why. I'm a perfectly good driver. I've been driving for years... But no, she had to drive. Three sets of traffic lights we went through. At least two halt signs and as for speed limits... My nerves, Ollie, for the last ten miles, they were literally screaming...
Oliver Couldn't have gone that fast. You're nearly an hour late as it is.
David That's only because we started *two* hours late. Can you imagine that? Trouble is, basically, it's not her fault. It's just that I'm no good for her. It's a terrible admission, but I'm not.
Oliver It doesn't sound as if she's doing you an awful lot of good, either.
David I let her down. In every way. I can see her—visibly being let down while I'm doing it. Why do I do it?

Jenny enters with a glass of water

Jenny Here you are.

David Bless you, Jen. (*He holds up the pill bottle*) These are the only things that do the trick. For me, anyway. Absolutely marvellous.

Jenny What are they?

David Para-hydrus-neutra-valisterin compound. Haven't you come across them?

Jenny No, they're new, aren't they?

David They keep me alive. They're wonderful for the nerves.

Jenny I must try them.

David They're a sedative, really.

Oliver Does that mean you're about to fall asleep?

David I wish to God I could. Polly's in an extraordinary mood. Wouldn't speak to me all the way down. Seventy miles an hour, just kept muttering to herself.

Oliver Muttering what?

David Don't know, couldn't hear half the time. Things like, "We'll settle that bitch once and for all." Things like that.

Jenny Who did she mean?

David How the hell should I know? You? Mother? Deirdre? Do you think she talks to me? As far as I can make out, she only keeps me around the house to open bottles and frighten burglars.

Oliver Are you effective?

Jenny Tea's nearly ready, anyway. I'm just going to fetch Father.

Jenny goes off upstairs

David I'll feel better in a minute. (*He makes for the table*) These are very fast-acting. (*At the table*) What are in these?

Oliver (*sourly*) Crab.

David Oh my God, that's the last straw. Everyone else arrived?

Oliver Yes. Deirdre's brought another bloke.

David Not another one of those?

Oliver No, he's quite presentable.

David Never forget Mother's face last time. She drew the curtains in the morning and saw them both sitting on the lawn absolutely stark naked, watching the sunrise.

Oliver I think her main worry was they'd get rheumatism.

David Well, this family's got quite enough problems without that.

Oliver Do you mean normally? Or are you referring to something special?

David Polly'll tell you. I couldn't begin.

Oliver Everyone's been dropping rather dark hints. I seem to be the only one who doesn't know.

David You will, don't worry, you will. We're leaking oil too.

Oliver Mmm?

David The car's leaking oil. We're getting through pints.
Oliver Better get it fixed.

Emma enters with a teapot

Emma Tea up. Hallo, David. Where's Polly?
David She's here.
Emma Jenny's gone up to fetch Father.
David How is he?
Emma Oh, well, I think. Very well.
Oliver What on earth does he get up to, in that room of his? I've often wondered.
Emma Well, I've never really dared ask him. He's very quiet about it, whatever it is, which is one blessing, I suppose. I think he just reads. Oliver, I wonder if you could give Deirdre and her young man a call?
Oliver Yes, of course. Tell them to put their clothes on and come in for tea.
Emma We're having no more of that, I can tell you.

Oliver goes out

We had a petition, you know, David, a petition. Dr and Mrs Cartwright from next door with fourteen signatures.
David But the garden isn't overlooked by that many people.
Emma Yes, dear, now come and sit down. Well, how are you both?
David Oh, pretty fair.
Emma Polly very busy, is she?
David Oh, yes, yes.
Emma She doesn't write very much these days.
David I wish she'd write to me occasionally as well. I see so little of her. She's been working evenings, you see.
Emma Evenings, too?
David Well, they had a rush job. Her boss asked her if she'd... She got overtime, of course.
Emma That's nice.

Jenny enters

Jenny He threw a book at me.
Emma What's that, dear?
Jenny Father. He threw a book at me. I put my head round the door and said, "Hallo, Father. Tea's ready. Don't be long, will you?" And he threw a book at me.
Emma Now I did tell you, dear, not to go in there. He doesn't like it. He never did. Just a little knock and then very gently, "Tea's made, Father".

Jenny But I'm his daughter, Mother. His daughter. If I can't even call him for his tea...

David From what I've heard, it's a good job you're not his wife.

Emma Now that's an uncalled for remark, David. What did you mean by that?

David Nothing.

Jenny (*nervously*) He didn't mean anything, Mother. Nothing at all.

David Nothing.

Emma Well, this is going to be a happy evening. I won't have any of you spoiling it. That includes you, David. I know we must make allowances because of your nerves, but all the same.

Oliver enters

Oliver They're coming in. Very respectable. Fully clothed and playing football on the lawn.

Emma Not the side lawn.

Oliver That's the one.

Emma I hope they didn't disturb Father. It's right under his window.

Oliver He'd no doubt have made his feelings known, if they had.

Jenny Your tea, Oliver.

Emma Pass round the sandwiches, too, dear. We won't wait for the others. Where on earth is Polly?

David In the garden, I think. She went to look at—something.

Emma Went to look at what?

David (*guiltily*) The greenhouse.

Emma The greenhouse? What on earth did she want to look at in the greenhouse?

As David opens his mouth to reply, Deirdre enters

Deirdre Ta-ra! Everyone, a presentation ceremony. Come in, Jas.

James enters with a large bunch of flowers

Speech by Jas.

James (*sheepishly*) On behalf of us both, Mrs Gray, to wish you and your husband a very happy anniversary.

Emma Oh, how lovely.

Deirdre Happy Anniversary, Ma.

Emma (*touched*) How absolutely lovely. Look everyone, what... Oh, my God! They're Father's.

Jenny ⎫   ⎰ Oh, no.
Oliver ⎬ (*together*) ⎨ Deirdre!
David ⎭   ⎱ Oh, good grief!
Emma Deirdre, you wicked girl. You knew these were Father's. He'll be absolutely furious.
Jenny You idiot.
Oliver He won't forget that in a hurry.
Deirdre What's the flap? He'll never miss a few.
Emma Of course he will. You know perfectly well he counts them every morning.
James I'm terribly sorry...
David Perhaps you could say it was a bird?
Oliver What sort of a bird? An eagle?
Emma I just don't know what we're going to do.
Jenny Oh, Mother...
David What about frost bite?
Jenny In August?
Emma Oh, do be quiet, David. Don't be so stupid. It'll be me that gets into trouble, you know. He adores you, Deirdre, you know that. It'll be me he'll blame.
Jenny I'll get rid of them, Mother. Here...
Emma No, I'll take them into the kitchen. Put them in some water and hide them somewhere, I suppose. There's just a chance he won't notice. You really are very naughty, dear.
James I'm awfully sorry. I had no idea.
Emma A very naughty girl indeed.

Emma goes out

Deirdre (*to James*) Told you you'd get a good reaction.
James Yes. Thanks a lot.
David Well, that's really done it, hasn't it? I mean, that's all we needed. The one thing we needed. We're in for a perfectly marvellous evening now, aren't we? (*To James*) How do you do, I'm David. Oh, my God. I've got indigestion.
Oliver Have a crab sandwich.
David I don't know why you're sitting there so smugly. You're the one we're relying on to sort this out.
Oliver Sort what out? I do wish someone would tell me exactly.
David You don't know? You don't know? Well, you must be about the only one who doesn't. (*He paces about*)

Polly, in her early thirties, smartly dressed, enters during the following

The only one. If you must know——
Polly Sit down, David, for heaven's sake. Stop flapping about.
Deirdre Ah, Madam's arrived.
Oliver At last.
Polly Hallo, Oliver, Jenny... (*She regards her with disapproval*) Oh, just look at you... Didn't you read *any* of those pamphlets I sent you?
Jenny Now listen, don't——
Polly Hallo, big D. You still growing too? (*To James*) Oh. Hallo.
James Hallo. James.
Polly Oh yes? Polly.
Oliver Now you've consented to arrive, perhaps I can be told what's going on?
Deirdre And me.
Polly Oh, hasn't he told you? It's fairly straightforward. Apparently Father has been trying, so far unsuccessfully, to kill Mother.

A pause

Oliver Good grief.
Deirdre Crikey!
David It's an incredible story, Ollie, I could hardly believe it, I——
Polly I'd better tell him, David. You'll only exaggerate and get it all wrong... (*She fishes in her handbag and produces a letter*) Last Thursday, I received this letter addressed to me from Mrs Cartwright. For those of you who don't know, she's our next door neighbour who owns that house just at the back of here.
Deirdre Snooper Cartwright. Mrs Longnose.
Polly In this particular case, perhaps it's just as well... Anyway, I'll read the letter... "Dear Polly, I am writing to you as my husband is not feeling up to corresponding at present. I hardly know how to write this but write it I must and I hope you will bear with me. Last Wednesday, I was cleaning my hall window that happens to overlook your garden——"
Deirdre We know which window that is.
Jenny The cleanest window in the house.
Polly "——overlook your garden, when I happened to glance up and see your mother in the greenhouse. She was staggering to and fro in what seemed to be a choking and gasping state..." (*She stares at the tea-table*) My God, she's made some more of those dreadful cakes.
Jenny Go on, go on.
Polly "...choking and gasping state, beating on the greenhouse door which was closed. I summoned my husband and we watched for a while in case there was a natural explanation. When you mother fell to her knees——"
David Fell to her knees. Did you hear that? Fell to her——

Polly (*sharply*) David, please don't interrupt when I'm reading. "When your mother fell to her knees we realized it was an emergency and immediately rushed to her assistance. All this time your mother's colour was deteriorating. Once in the fresh air, Mrs Gray revived, but upon investigation my husband discovered that the reason for her condition had been that the heating control had been set by someone at a dangerously high level." Capital letters.

David (*under his breath*) Capital letters.

Polly "Strangely, your father throughout all this had heard nothing from his study and when we later informed him of your mother's narrow escape seemed completely unconcerned. Whilst I hope you don't feel I am drawing conclusions from this, I felt that you should be informed" ... etcetera etcetera.

Deirdre Blimey.

David I shan't be able to eat a thing tonight.

Oliver Could have been an accident, I suppose.

Jenny It doesn't sound like one.

Deirdre Old Mother Cartwright probably made it all up, knowing her.

Jenny Oh, don't be so silly.

Oliver I suppose we ought to have it out with them both. Get to the bottom of it.

Deirdre Good luck.

Oliver (*doubtfully*) Yes.

Jenny The pressure cooker blew up too, you know. Mother told me. There's a dent in the kitchen ceiling. Do you think he...?

Oliver Mother does that sort of thing regularly. That ceiling's positively worn away by exploding tins.

Jenny To think that we gave it to her, Oliver, for Christmas.

Oliver Simmer down, Jenny.

Deirdre Well, what fun. (*To James*) Enjoying yourself?

Polly (*to James*) Sorry to involve you in all this. Whoever you are.

Deirdre Mine. Hands off.

Polly You're certainly a cut above Deirdre's average.

Jenny Someone's got to do something. Mother's in great danger. I mean, he's probably up there at the moment building bombs.

David The question, as I see it, is how to stop this getting out of hand.

Polly (*applauding him*) Brilliant.

Jenny She's got to be protected from that man. It's a fine thing when one's own mother isn't safe in her own house. With her own husband.

Polly Or put it another way. It's a fine thing when one's own father is reduced to trying to murder his wife out of sheer desperation.

David You're not saying that this is Mother's fault?

Polly Of course it is. If he's trying to kill her off, she's no-one to blame but

rself. It's just his way of saying thank you for years of utterly miserable
...arriage.

Deirdre Bloody hell. Isn't she marvellous?

Jenny This is absolutely outrageous. I won't listen to this; how can you be
so disloyal to Mother?

Polly Or you to Father.

Jenny He's virtually a murderer.

Polly He's a long-term victim of that stupid bitch in the kitchen.

Jenny How dare you?

Oliver Oy, oy, oy.

David (*urgently*) Ssh.

Emma comes in

Emma I've put them at the back of the china cabinet. I don't think he'll find
them there... Oh, Polly, how nice. At last.

Polly Mother.

Emma Now then, has everybody got their tea? No, Polly hasn't got one.
That's not like you, Polly. You usually make straight for the teapot. What
was it we used to say, Jenny, whenever Polly came home from school?

Deirdre (*dully*) "Polly put the kettle on".

Emma "Polly put the kettle on", that's right. (*She laughs*) I hope you're all
admiring my new teaspoons. From Oliver and Jenny. (*She pours tea*)

David hiccups and mutters. A silence

Here we are, Polly. (*She sits*) Well, isn't this lovely? All of you here
together. My three little girls, all with your young men. Polly and David,
Jenny and Oliver, little Deirdre and—er, Jas.

An embarrassed silence

Isn't it quiet? What is it they say? There's an angel passing overhead.

*Edward enters from the kitchen, clutching the flowers in his fist. He looks
round threateningly as——*

Black-out

The same. A second later

Only the individual relationships have changed. Oliver is now married to Deirdre, David to Jenny who is still pregnant, and James has been invited down by Polly. The relative physical positioning of each pair has correspondingly altered since the end of Scene 1. The clothes, particularly the women's, have also changed, reflecting the new relationships. They are all, though, basically the same people merely altered by the different circumstances of their lives. David and Jenny are poorer since David, under her influence, is more unsuccessful than ever. Deirdre is happily spending Oliver's money and it shows. Polly is more the bachelor girl making less compromises than ever. James is still James, but now wears trousers. Edward remains unfortunately married to Emma

Emma Well, isn't this lovely? All of you here together. My three little girls, all with your young men. Jenny and David, little Deirdre and Oliver, and Polly and—er, James.

An embarrassed silence

Isn't it quiet? What is it they say? There's an angel passing overhead.

Edward enters from the kitchen with the flowers

Edward And which of you miserable half-wits is responsible for this?

A pause

Emma Well, I'm afraid it was me actually, Father.
Edward (*mystified*) You?
Emma Yes. It was very silly of me. I hadn't got my glasses so I didn't notice that they were your specials.
Edward And presumably, still without your glasses, you brought them indoors, put them in water and then stuffed them in the back of the china cupboard?
Emma No, Father, not exactly——
Edward It was one of this lot. You're covering up as usual, Emma. And we know who that's usually in aid of, don't we?
Deirdre Hallo, Father.
Edward Well?
Deirdre Yes, Father. Well you see, I walked into the garden and there they were, so beautiful and innocent... I was suddenly overcome...

Oliver (*muttering*) Oh, good grief.
Deirdre I stood right next to them, Father, and then the thought came to me. I want to run with them into the house, rush into this room and let everyone share them. And suddenly, on a mad impulse, I picked them.
Oliver (*muttering*) You're overdoing it.
Deirdre I'm awfully sorry, Father. Really.
Edward (*after a pause, roaring and aiming a wild cuff at her head which she ducks*) You damn liar!
Emma Father! You can see she's very upset—I'll pop them in some water, dear. Give them to me.
Deirdre No, I'll do it, Mother.
Emma No, dear, I'll——
Edward Let her do it, Emma. The least she can do under the circumstances.
Deirdre It's the least I can do, Mother. (*She takes the flowers from Emma*)
Edward And this time, don't stick them in the back of a cupboard. Let's have them on show somewhere.

Deirdre exits during the following

Then we can all sit round and watch them die. Still unable to keep your wife under control, Oliver.
Oliver Never could, Edward. No better than anyone else ever could, anyway. Deirdre's not really governed by natural laws.
Edward Only thing to do with a wife like that is to keep her on a chain.
Emma Father! Your tea.
Edward Thank you, dear.
Emma Polly dear, Father's chair.
Polly (*rising*) Sorry, my mistake.
Edward (*seeing James*) I don't think we've met.
James James.
Edward James?
Emma This is Polly's young man.
Edward Polly's?
Emma Down for the weekend, dear.
Edward With Polly?
Polly Yes.
Edward Poor devil!
Polly Thank you.
Edward Well, how's everyone?

Everyone murmurs "fine"

You're looking pasty, David. Not enough fresh air? Wife been overfeeding you? You're both looking decidedly flabby.

Emma There's an excuse for Jenny, Father.

Edward Oh, yes? What's that? Good God, you're not having another one, are you?

Emma Father! You know she is.

Edward I can't keep up with her.

Polly Hear, hear.

Edward Still, he's not having one. No excuse for him. Cut his diet to a quarter, send him off for walks, he might see the other side of forty. Buy him a greyhound or something to run after.

Jenny (*huffily*) We could hardly afford one and David's already on a very strict diet.

David (*apologetically*) Touch of the old stomach trouble again. Nothing serious.

Edward That's what they all say.

David What?

Edward Tommy Granger used to say that, didn't he, Emma, "nothing serious"? Sitting there, clutching his stomach, nearly falling off the settee in agony and stuffing himself with home-made cake. "Nothing serious", he'd say. Still saying that when they nailed him down.

David Oh, my God.

Emma Yes, wasn't that sad? And old Mrs Lamb from the village, did I tell you, Jenny, she passed away at last. One minute she was walking around and the next...

Edward Dead as mutton.

Emma Very sudden.

Edward Quick and clean.

Emma Better that way.

Edward Much better.

Oliver Mother, any chance of something to eat?

Emma Oh, yes. Now then, Father, something to eat? Oh, I haven't put out your special sandwiches. Jenny, we forgot Father's special sandwiches.

Oliver What's this, preferential treatment?

Emma He's found ordinary butter doesn't agree with him.

Edward Not the butter you buy. Don't know where you get it.

Emma Brought him out in a terrible rash. Really terrible.

Edward There's no need to exaggerate, it wasn't that bad.

David That's what they all say.

Edward glares at him

Deirdre enters with the flowers in a plain vase

Deirdre Here we are.

Emma Oh darling, you should have used that pretty cut-glass vase. The one that Auntie Susan...
Deirdre Well... Mother... Ha, ha—a funny thing happened on my way to the sink with it.
Emma Deirdre, you didn't.
Edward Every damn thing she touches...
Emma Deirdre, I loved that vase, too.
Deirdre Never mind. Oliver will buy you another.

Oliver laughs mirthlessly

Emma (*making for the kitchen*) That's not the point. Auntie Susan brought that back from Pitlochry.

Emma goes out to the kitchen

Edward Those boys of yours, Jenny...
Jenny Yes, Father.
Edward I've got some toy soldiers for them. Had them for ages. I'll look them out.
Deirdre I didn't know you played soldiers, Father.
Edward Not for me. Bought them when your Mother was expecting Polly. Wishful thinking on my part.
Polly Sorry to disappoint you, Father.
Edward Your lads might like them. Didn't bring them this time, did you?
Jenny (*livening*) No, well, we couldn't. What with us going out tonight. I asked Mrs Greaves if she'd sit in and she very kindly... They should be all right with her, though Jason's always terrible when we leave him. I mean, I think he really does need continual affection, doesn't he, David?
David Yes, he does, he really does.
Jenny Quite the reverse of Mark, who's almost unaffectionate, isn't he, David?
David Yes. Yes, I think it's probably a phase.
Jenny He hasn't got little Jason's nature at all. Jason's so cheerful, never been any trouble.
David Never. What worries me about Mark is all this crying in corners. If he'd only come and talk it over, tell me what's worrying him.
Jenny Still, he's only four, darling.
David He can still come and talk it over. He's a human being, for God's sake. I'm a human being.
Jenny He's still bed-wetting, too.
Edward Oh, dear.
Jenny In fact, if anything, it's getting worse. There was one night—it was what? Three times, wasn't it, David?

David At least, yes.

Jenny We ran out of sheets. I was up twice and the third time I said, "David, I just can't get up any more".

David It doesn't seem to matter how many times we pot him, either.

A pause

Edward But they're all right apart from that?

Jenny Oh, fine. David's made a video of them.

Deirdre Of Mark on the pot. How super. Can't wait to see that.

Jenny It's all very well for you to laugh, Deirdre. You wait till you and Oliver eventually have children, you'll find it's not all plain sailing. You try being woken up at three in the morning, day in, day out.

Deirdre When Oliver and I decide on a family, the first thing I shall get is an au pair.

Oliver Prefer that to a child, I must say.

Deirdre laughs

Jenny Personally, I think no marriage is complete without children. I don't know how people can stay married and not have children.

Deirdre It's very easy, darling, remind me to tell you all about it some time.

Edward That's enough of that, if you don't mind. I won't have smutty talk under my roof, not even from you.

Deirdre Pardon.

Polly Well, at the risk of being sent up to my room with only bread and water, I must say I rather admire people who decide not to have children.

Edward I don't know where the devil your Mother's got to with my sandwiches.

Polly (*ploughing on*) I think it's very admirable.

James You mean over-population and so on?

Edward Good God. He spoke.

Deirdre Don't get her started on over-population—we'll be here for ever.

Polly For once I wasn't talking about that. I was talking about people having children who weren't really fit to cope with them.

Jenny If you're referring to David and me, I take that as a...

Polly I don't know why you should feel I was doing that, Jenny.

Jenny I'm sick and tired of putting up with you sneering every time——

Polly (*innocently*) What did I say?

Jenny We don't sit around discussing your personal life, you know.

Polly (*amused*) What have I said?

Jenny I mean, there's a lot of things... I mean, I may have children but at least I'm not a cradle snatcher.

Oliver Jenny.
Edward Hey-hey-hey.
Polly (*dangerous*) A what?
Jenny Makes a change from fat old men, I suppose.
Polly Shut up.
James Fat old men?
Deirdre Just a sisterly joke, James.
Edward Enough.
Deirdre Anyway, talking of men being fat...
Edward (*roaring her down*) I said that's enough!

A silence

> What's the matter with this family? Can't even get a cup of tea in peace.
> You three women are just about the blind limit, aren't you? In all my life,
> I have never seen or heard three more neurotic, bitchy, discontented
> females.

Polly My point exactly, Father.
Edward Um?
Polly There are certain couples totally unsuited to bring up children.

A pause

Edward (*menacingly*) Do I understand you correctly, young lady?
David The new video of the children came out awfully well, didn't it, Jen?
Edward Did I understand you correctly?
Polly I think you did.
David A bit out of focus in parts.
Edward You have the brazen impudence to sit there in my house ... under
my roof...

Deirdre starts to sing

> And tell me to my face... When I think of the sacrifices that your Mother—
> will you shut up, Deirdre—the sacrifices that your Mother and I have
> made.

Polly Here we go. He's at the clichés.
Edward Don't walk away when I'm talking to you.
Polly Clichés! Clichés!
Edward If you're not careful, my girl, I'll...
Polly Don't threaten me, Father. I do have a gallant escort who would no
doubt leap to my aid. Wouldn't you, James?
James I...

Edward Oh, yes? What have you got to say for yourself?

Polly Don't frighten him, Father.

Edward (*to James*) You take my tip, you head for that front door and start running. Before you find yourself married to her.

Polly I'm sure James has no intention of marrying me.

Edward Not if he's any sense.

Polly What is it you're always saying, Father. We all marry the wrong people, isn't that it?

Oliver Polly.

Polly Now, what I'd love to know is, would you include your own marriage in that category, Father?

Edward If you think I'm going to discuss my...

Polly Because if you do, what course of action would you take supposing you discovered you had married the wrong person?

Edward Eh?

Oliver Polly.

Deirdre I volunteer to dispose of Mummy's Delights.

Polly Divorce? No. Think of the effect on the children.

Deirdre Paper bag? Anyone got a paper bag?

Polly How would you set about dissolving an unsuccessful partnership?

Edward What?

Deirdre (*finding a bag and reaching inside*) Ah!

Jenny Don't take any notice of her, Father—Deirdre, that's my knitting!

Deirdre (*taking knitting out of the bag and starting to load it with cakes*) Bad luck.

Jenny Anyway, what does she know about marriage?

Polly Well, Father?

Jenny When you've been married as long as David and I have, you'll...

Deirdre Ta-rah! Introducing the case of the nervous night nurse.

Polly Father?

Deirdre She was so frightened of the dark she had to get into bed with her patient.

Jenny How dare you!

David She didn't.

Edward Quiet!

Deirdre A truly great love story. *In* went the thermometer, *up* went his temperature, and *down* came her nursing knickers.

Edward Right. That's it. Out. Out. I won't have talk like that in my house, I don't care how old you are.

Deirdre Pa...

Edward Get out.

Deirdre (*retreating to the stairs*) Pa... (*She throws the bag of cakes to Jenny*) Here!

ard *Out!*
Deirdre (*going upstairs*) Banished! Banished!

Deirdre exits

A pause

Edward You were saying, Polly?
Polly Was I, Father?
Edward Come on. Don't try and duck out of it now. You were saying...?
There are some...? Come on. There are some people who aren't fit to bring
up children. Was that it? Eh?
Polly That'll do for a start, Father.
Edward Then perhaps you'd like to explain that remark. I'd like to hear——
Jenny Now, Father, why don't you sit down with us and I'll pour you a nice
fresh cup of tea. David and I have some lovely pictures of our holiday in
Climping. I'm sure you'd love——
Edward Will you be quiet! I want to hear what this girl has to say.
Jenny All right. All right. I'm certainly not sitting here to be insulted by her
and shouted at by my own father. Here. (*She gives the bag of cakes to Polly*)
David Jenny.
Jenny (*going upstairs*) I've done all I can. If it isn't enough, I'm sorry. That's
all. I can't do any more.

Jenny goes off upstairs

Polly It's thinning out.
Edward You ought to be damn well ashamed of yourself, young woman.
Polly Language, Father.
Edward You of all people ought to know better. I expect that sort of
behaviour from that lot. (*He moves to the stairs*)
Polly Don't you want to hear what I had to say now, Father?
Edward No, I don't. Jenny's absolutely right. You just sit there stirring
things up, that's all.
Polly There's usually a reason for it.
Edward (*to James*) I only hope you know what you've got yourself into with
her, young man. That's all I can say.

Edward exits upstairs

Polly (*pleased*) Hah! Well, if you'll excuse me, gentlemen, I must just go
and make myself lovely before we go on our little outing. (*She gives the
knitting bag to James*) Get rid of these, will you?

Polly exits upstairs

change ito
(Deirdre)
Penny (uncrumpled)
evening dress

The three men stand awkwardly. A silence

David I don't know what all that fuss was about. I really don't. I was an outpatient.
Oliver Ah!

Another silence

I'll tell you something. We really ought to get things straight with Mother before we go out to dinner.
David Get what straight?
Oliver All this—potting shed business.
David The greenhouse.
Oliver Yes.
David See if we can help.
Oliver Yes. Better make it quick too. It's going to be a race between our guiding hand and Polly's boot.
David Oh, good grief.
Oliver (*to James*) I certainly take my hat off to you, coping with her.

Emma enters with Edward's sandwiches on a plate

Emma Deirdre, you naughty girl. You made a terrible mess out there. Broken vases, flower petals… Oh. (*She sees the depleted gathering*) Where's everyone gone?
Oliver (*lamely*) We're still here.
Emma Yes, but where's everyone? Have they finished?
James I think—they dashed off to change.
Oliver Yes, they dashed off…
David To change.
Emma Oh. Well, perhaps that's just as well. It's about time we had one of our heart to hearts, don't you think? Just the men.
Oliver (*dismayed*) Oh.
David (*dismayed*) Ah.
Emma We have these from time to time, James. We all find it can be very helpful. Of course, they're all wonderful girls but that doesn't mean they can't be … at times.
Oliver Better keep an eye on the clock, Mother.
Emma Yes, dear. And how are you and little Deirdre? Everything all right?
Oliver Absolutely marvellous, Mother. Sheer bliss.
Emma Really?

Oliver Never been happier.
Emma (*disappointed*) Oh. Good. And, David, what...?
David (*hastily*) Wonderful ... wonderful.
Emma And Jenny?
David Wonderful.
Oliver I'd have said, Mother, that David and I have got a pretty clean bill of health. Wouldn't you say so, David?
David Oh, yes. Absolutely.
Oliver If you're looking for someone with problems, I don't think you need look any further than ... er... (*He looks towards James*)

David follows his lead and does likewise

Emma (*looking at James*) Oh.
James Sorry?
Emma (*sympathetically*) Problems, James?
James Problems?
Emma With Polly?
James Polly... Er, no ... no... Not really.
Emma (*turning to the others*) Oh, dear. It sounds like the same old story, doesn't it?
David Same old story.
Emma If you knew the sleepless nights Edward and I have had over that girl, James.
David I should think he's had one or two of those.
Emma What's that, dear?
David Nothing, nothing.
Emma Well, don't mutter, David. You're always muttering these days.
David Sorry.
Emma Yes, dear. Well, it's a good job James wasn't here last year, Oliver. With ... er...
Oliver Ah, yes.
Emma Him.
David The fat man?
Emma Say no more, dear. Say no more.
David No, no, no.
James The fat, old man you mean?
Emma Ah. You know?
James A little.
Oliver I thought he was a rather decent sort of chap, you know. Good sense of humour. Told us that marvellous one about the...
Emma Until his wife turned up with their children, right in the middle of breakfast.

Oliver Oh, good Lord, that's right. The blonde woman.

Emma Tinted, of course, but beautifully set. They were gorgeous children though, James. So well-behaved. Always please this and thank you that.

Oliver Please can we have our Daddy back. Thank you.

David Was he the one who showed us that nasty scar?

Emma No, that was the year before. That was her man from Wormwood Scrubs. He was quite different. Threatening Edward, like that... (*To James*) You're a most welcome change, dear.

James Thank you.

Emma I shudder to think who she'll bring next year.

David If there is a next year.

Emma Now, that's very gloomy, David.

David Sorry.

Emma Yes, well, try and be a little jollier.

Oliver Mother, now we've got you on your own—we'd rather welcome a word with you, actually.

Emma Oh, really?

Oliver Wouldn't we, David?

David What?

Oliver A word. With Mother.

David Oh, yes. Yes.

James (*tentatively rising, offering to leave*) Should I...

Oliver No, no, stay here. That's all right.

Emma What's all this? A secret?

Oliver Not at all, Mother. We were just all of us wondering, in a general sort of way, how you and Edward were managing, so far as the question of getting along together was concerned, to ... er ... get along. Together.

Emma (*confused*) Well...

Oliver I hope you don't mind my asking.

Emma I'm just not quite sure what you're asking.

David We're asking, how are you?

Emma Very well, thank you.

David Good.

Oliver Grand. Both of you keeping fit? That sort of thing?

Emma Yes. Edward's had a twinge of his... You know.

Oliver Ah——

Emma But nothing his tablets can't put right.

Oliver Good.

Emma And I ... just occasionally. But only when it's damp.

David Grand.

Oliver So, you're both managing to keep pretty sound in body and—er...

David Mind.

Emma What's that, dear?

David Mind. How you go. (*He pauses*) With the time.

Emma Oh yes, heavens, we mustn't be late. We've got a long drive.

Oliver Yes. Just before you dash off, Emma. All's quiet on the home front, then?

Emma Oh, yes, dear.

Oliver Grand.

Emma Quiet as the grave.

David What?

Oliver Splendid. Yes. Well, that's all we were concerned about. Grand. False alarm then.

Emma False alarm?

Oliver Oh, it was just there was some idiótic rumour... It's not important, Emma. Don't worry about it.

Emma Rumour? About me?

Oliver No, it's not worth mentioning, Emma.

David Nothing, nothing.

Oliver Concerned Edward more than you, really.

Emma Edward? Rumours about Edward?

Oliver Well, I mean, with the greatest respect, Emma, the old boy does seem to get odder the older he gets.

Emma Oh, I don't think he does. He always was rather—odd—if you can call it that. Even as a young man.

David Ah!

Oliver Really?

Emma Oh, yes. Even we had our little problems, to start with.

David Ah!

Oliver Anything—at all significant, Mother?

Emma Not really. I remember he was never very fond of women, for some reason.

David Ah!

Emma Oh, do stop saying "ah" like that, David, it's terribly irritating. I mean, when I say Edward wasn't fond of women... It wasn't that he didn't like them. He was perfectly healthy. He just didn't want them around. Which made it very difficult. When I was courting him, that is...

Oliver How did you manage to net him? Disguise yourself as a dahlia?

Emma Well, I must confess I did rather set my cap at him. Luckily, he didn't seem to mind me quite so much. He used to tell me I was one of the chaps. Which from him was quite a compliment, believe me.

Oliver Not very gallant.

Emma Oh, no, he used to hold doors open for me and things like that. Walk on the outside of the pavement. If he wasn't in a hurry. Mind you, he usually was in those days. He loved walking. Then we both did. That's how we met. Walking.

David From different directions, you mean?

Emma (*slightly irritably*) No, dear, hiking. He used to come round to my house, knock on the door, pick me up and away we'd go. Hiking for miles and miles.

David What did you do when it rained?

Emma Well, he didn't come round, dear, did he? Don't be so silly.

Oliver Good way to get to know someone. Hiking together.

Emma Oh, I don't think he ever said very much. Except things like, "Now where the devil are we?" He was hopeless with maps, you see. We usually went in huge circles. Round and round. I could barely keep up with him. He refused to stop and ask, you see. We just kept on going. He can never be still. Even to this day. If Edward and I ever do find ourselves sitting down together, up he gets, off he goes. I think that's what attracted me to him, really. I do admire active men.

Oliver Always depending on their course of action, that is.

Emma But then, Edward and I are a perfect example of what I've always said about marriage. It doesn't matter who you are, in this life, when you finally get married it's bound to be to someone you really deserve.

Oliver That's a pretty withering indictment, Mother.

Polly appears on the landing during the following, and listens, unseen. She is wearing evening clothes

Emma And if they do have little shortcomings—then take a close look at yourself. Because you probably have them, too. And it's up to both of you to help each other. It's the easiest thing in the world to run away—but that's not the answer. That's no solution.

Polly Stay and fight it out to the death? Is that what you're saying, Mother?

David Oh, my God.

Oliver Polly!

Emma Oh, Polly, dear.

Oliver Good gracious me, Mother. Sorry to break things up, but have you seen the time?

David Oh, yes, yes. Good heavens.

Oliver Must have a quick splash over, before we go.

David I must look at the car ... that oil leak.

Oliver You'd better get a move on too, Emma. Excuse us.

David Excuse us.

David and Oliver go out

Emma (*moving to go herself*) Yes, well, I suppose we'd—oh, look! All those little cakes of mine. All gone. The children call them Mummy's Delights, you know, James.

James (*clutching the bag to him*) Ah——
Emma What's that you're clutching, dear? It looks like Jenny's little knitting
  bag.
James Er——
Emma (*taking it from him*) Give it to me, I'll take it up to her when I go.
  Otherwise someone will sit on it.

Emma goes out

James My God.
Polly What's wrong? Been exposed to an overdose of family?
James Wrong? You invite me down for a quiet weekend and then, without
  any warning at all ... that letter. I mean, why didn't you tell me you'd had
  a letter like that——
Polly I didn't think you'd be all that interested in my family trivia.
James I think I ought to leave now.
Polly Well, that's up to you, of course.

Deirdre enters. She wears a new and obviously expensive dress

You'll miss all the fun if you do.
Deirdre Hallo, love-birds. (*To James*) Has she been getting at you, now?
Polly Not at all.
Deirdre Whatever she's been telling you, James, don't believe a word of it.
  (*Displaying the dress*) Well?
Polly What?
Deirdre Do you like it?
Polly Breathtaking.
Deirdre Got it today when Ollie's back was turned.
Polly That must have cost him a bit.
Deirdre Probably.
Polly How much?
Deirdre I didn't look. It's rude to read other people's bills. Ask Ollie.
Polly He'll get wise to you one day.
Deirdre Why should he? I treat him very well.
Polly Good for you.
Deirdre Couple of the year. That's us.
Polly If you ever do get bored you can always try David.
Deirdre David?
Polly Think of the challenge. Every time you woke up in the morning beside
  him and found he was still breathing you'd feel a personal sense of triumph.

They laugh. They stop as they see James

Someone's not amused.
Deirdre Does he smile at all—or is he stuck like that?
Polly No. He's been known to smile. In fact he's got quite a repertoire once
you get him started. You'd be surprised.
Deirdre Really? Tell me more.
James I'm sorry. I feel there are some things that are too important to joke
about.

The girls coo in chorus

Deirdre Really. Name six.

David enters from the front door

David The big end's gone.
Polly What?
David I've just had a look at the car and the big end's gone. Oh God, now
what? How the hell are we going to get there? I ask you? How the hell...?
I need a pill. I must have a pill. (*He feels in his pockets*) Damn, Jenny's got
them. (*He calls*) Jenny! Jenny!

Jenny enters hurriedly from upstairs

Jenny What's that, dear?
Deirdre Give him a pill, his big end's gone.
Jenny Oh, darling, where?
David Give me a pill. Just give me one of my pills. The red ones.

Oliver enters

Oliver Here we are, then. All ready?
David Ollie. My God, that damn car——
Oliver Oh, yes—find out what it was, did you?
David The big end——
Oliver (*laughing*) Bad luck.
David Pills, darling—where are the pills?
Jenny (*suddenly impatient*) Just a minute, darling. Here. (*She hands him
some pills*)
David Thank you. Water—no water.

David goes into the kitchen

Jenny Oh, well, I think I'll start clearing while we're waiting.

Deirdre There's one here. (*She hands Jenny a plate she's missed*)
Jenny Father's sandwiches. I wonder if he wants them.
Polly I doubt it.
Deirdre We could always take them in a polythene bag.
Polly Yes, he'll probably hate the menu there.
Jenny Father and foreign cooking.

David comes back with a glass of water, holding the pills

(*Examining the sandwich*) He's got this terrible thing about vegetarian
margarine. He claims he can't ... ouch!
Polly What's the matter?
Jenny Nothing, cut myself on the sandwich, that's all.
Polly Oh.

A pause

James Cut yourself on the sandwich?
Jenny Yes, it was sharp, I——
Oliver Let me see that.

They all converge on the plate

Good grief...
Deirdre What is it?
Oliver It's full of glass.
James Cut glass.
Jenny But who could have...?
Polly Well, now.

A silence

David I don't think I can bear this. They're both at it. I—can't bear it, I just
can't bear it.
Jenny Steady, David darling, steady.
Deirdre (*urgently*) Look out!

*They scatter as Emma and Edward enter arm in arm, both now dressed for
their evening out*

Oliver keeps hold of the plate, which he hides

Emma (*beaming round*) Oh, don't you all look pretty. Deirdre, that's really
lovely.

Deirdre smiles but can't speak

   Well now, is everybody ready?
Polly (*after a pause, uncertainly*) Ready, Mother.
Emma Oh, good. I must say, we're both really looking forward to this
  evening. Aren't we, Edward? Come along, everybody.

*Oliver passes the plate to David, who passes it to James, who is left standing
bewildered as——*

Black-out

(handwritten: Penny (Deirdre). Change out of evening dress)

ACT II

SCENE 1

The same. Later that evening

The partners have again changed. Polly is now married to Oliver, their two rather obstinate personalities meeting head-on. David is now overwhelmed by his wife Deirdre, she treating him like an exasperated parent with a backward child. James is now with Jenny who, while in no fit state to entertain amorous men, is still pregnant

Deirdre enters. She is very drunk and has David's coat over her shoulders

Deirdre Home sweet home. (*She nearly falls over the furniture. She tries to take off the coat and finishes up sitting on the settee with her arms still through one sleeve. She surveys the room*) Would whoever it is who's swinging on this room stop at once? This is my parents' house and they do not like their room swung on.

Emma, James and Jenny enter

Ma, someone is deliberately swinging your room.

Emma As for you, young lady——

Jenny Mother, sit down and let me...

Emma I have never been so embarrassed. What on earth did you children think you were up to? Thank you very much for the ride, James. You drove very nicely. A little too fast perhaps, but very nicely.

Jenny Mother, I'll get the coffee for us and——

Emma That's enough, Jenny. I don't want to hear another word. What an evening! Those people turning round at the next table and staring and the waiter having to speak to Father.

Deirdre It was a marvellous evening, marvellous food, marvellous company, marvellous bloody wine.

Emma Deirdre!

Deirdre Do you think Ollie's crashed his car?

Jenny Don't make jokes like that.

Deirdre Well, he started twenty minutes before we did. Mind you, he and Polly were having a great punch-up deciding who was going to drive.

Emma Deirdre, that will do. You're very over-excited, you're obviously not used to it. I'll make us some coffee.
Jenny I'll do it, Mother.
Emma No, you sit down, Jenny. Entertain your guest. I prefer to do it myself. I don't feel any of you are to be trusted just at the moment.

Emma goes out

Deirdre Where's that wet husband of mine? Has anyone seen damp David? Damp, dismal, dizzy David?
Jenny David couldn't help it. He was overcome by the heat.
Deirdre Fainting in the middle of dinner. *(She laughs)* I'll never forget him. More wine, David dear, and crash, over he goes, his feet sticking up in the air like...
Jenny It wasn't funny.
Deirdre I thought it was funny. I laughed.
Jenny We heard. It wouldn't hurt you to have travelled home with him either. He might have needed looking after.
Deirdre It's not my job to trail after him like a dog. I don't happen to be one of those women with canine instincts, man's best friend is his wife. Woof, woof, down girl. Lying on my back begging for the house-keeping money. *(She regards them)* All right, all right, I'm going. I can take a hint, I'm going.
Jenny Where?
Deirdre To help Mother. You're not the only one who can help Mother; I'm very good at helping Mother. I'll help her grind up some more glass for the coffee.
Jenny Deirdre, will you stop joking about it?

Deirdre goes out into the kitchen

I should be out there helping Mother, Deirdre's in no fit state.
James Jen...
Jenny No fit state. When I think of the time and trouble I took to arrange this evening, it really is sickening.
James Jen...

Polly enters from the front door without a word. She thumps her handbag hard against the furniture and sits

Hallo. You got back then?
Jenny It's pointless talking to her at the moment. We all know that mood when we see it.

James Jen...
Jenny (*irritated*) What is it, Jimmy?
James When do you think I ought to have a word with your father?
Jenny What about?
James Us. That's what I came down for, wasn't it?
Jenny How can we seriously think about marriage now? After what's happened?
James Happened?
Jenny With Mother and Father, for heaven's sake.
James But that's all the more reason why you need me here, Jen. To stand by you—and our baby. (*He touches her stomach affectionately*) If you're worried about your parents, then obviously——
Jenny Worried? I'm physically sick with apprehension. Sick.
Polly (*muttering*) I should never have married that man. Never. He has the mind of a sponge, the sensitivity of a brick wall and the manners of a pig.
Jenny No-one else is making the least effort ... not one of them.

Edward enters from the front door grimly

James Excuse me, sir, Jenny and I were wondering...

Edward strides past him to the kitchen door

Jenny Father, please, could we——
Edward Certainly not.

Edward goes out to the kitchen, slamming the door

Jenny I'm sorry, Jimmy, but as things are now, I couldn't consider marrying you—or anyone else.
James But why, Jen? God, ever since you've come back to this house you've hardly seemed to notice me. Why? After all we've been through together?
Jenny One night, Jimmy. That's all we really had. One night.
James It's a night I'll never forget, Jenny, as long as I live.
Jenny No. Nor will I.

Oliver enters from the front door, supporting David

Oliver Could you give me a hand?
James Jen...
Oliver I say, old boy, could you give me a hand?
James Oh God, what a house. (*He assists Oliver with David*)
Oliver Just put him here. He'll be all right in a minute.

David Yes, I'll be all right in a minute. Just the heat in that car after the restaurant.

James returns to Jenny

James Jen——
Jenny I'm their daughter, Jimmy. Their flesh and blood. Whatever they are, I am.
David And Deirdre's behaviour. It was so embarrassing. Didn't you find Deirdre embarrassing?
Oliver I don't think anybody noticed, old boy.
David Didn't notice? There was a crowd gathering in the street outside watching us eat.
Jenny If we got married now, how do you know in six months I wouldn't be trying to kill you?
James Well, marriage is always a risk, Jen. I'm prepared to risk it.
David I sat there thinking, my God, that's my wife.
Oliver I know the feeling. Can I get you a pill or something?
James Jen.
David Oh, thank you. Deirdre's got them somewhere, I think.
Jenny Go away, Jimmy.
James Jen.
Oliver Wherever she is.
Jenny Please.
James And leave you and the baby?
Oliver (*yelling*) Deirdre!
James Our baby?
Jenny She's in the kitchen helping Mother.
David What's got into her?
James Jen——
Polly She must be drunk. Like my husband.
Oliver (*calling*) Deirdre, Deirdre.
Polly Just look at him, will you?
Jenny Go away, Jimmy. For your own sake. Before it's too late.
James (*a sudden outburst*) I won't, Jen. I won't. I won't!

The others stare

Oliver Are we—er—in the way?
Jenny No.

Pause

Oliver Sure?

Jenny Yes.
Oliver Anything we can do?
Jenny No. Nothing at all.
Polly Please don't hesitate to make use of Uncle Oliver's Public Help Service. Public, of course. He'd never dream of doing it in private.
Oliver I really am going to lose my temper with you in a minute.
David Oh no, don't start again, please.
Polly It's all right, David, he won't dare do anything with you two here.
Oliver Oh, do shut up.
Polly He only dares lash out at home when we're alone. Then he spends the rest of the night pleading with me to tell people I'd walked into a cupboard door.
Oliver Polly...
Polly They must think I'm mentally defective at work. I seem to spend my evenings walking into cupboards.
David Could somebody ask Deirdre to fetch my pills, please?
Oliver I hit you once—purely in self defence.
Polly (*jeering*) Self defence!
David I'm finding it terribly hard to breathe.
Oliver Oh, good grief. (*He calls*) Deirdre.

Deirdre lurches in with a trayful of cups

Deirdre Coming. Here coffs the cuffy... I mean, here comes the coffee. (*She staggers*)
Jenny Get the tray.
Oliver Steady. (*He grabs it*)
Deirdre Thank you kindly.
Jenny Nearly Mother's carpet.
David Please, Deirdre. Try and behave with a little dignity. Just a little, please.

Deirdre tosses his coat which is still round her shoulders over David's head. During the following section, David puts it on

Oliver (*to Deirdre*) You'd better sit down before you fall down.
Deirdre Ha! Look who's talking.
Polly Hear, hear.
Oliver (*muttering*) I don't know why everyone persists in saying I'm drunk.
Deirdre (*sprawling on to settee*) That's better.
David Why can't my wife be dignified? Other people's wives are dignified. Other people take their wives out and introduce them to other people. I've seen them do it. I can't do that. I have to hide—behind potted ferns and coat stands. Waiting for somebody to carry her home——

Deirdre What are you muttering about?

David Deirdre, for heaven's sake, have you got my pills somewhere?

Deirdre Pills?

David Yes dear, the pills. My pills.

Deirdre Somewhere, probably. I'll have a look in a minute.

David I need them now.

Deirdre Then you'll have to get them yourself. They're in my handbag wherever that is.

Jenny Here!

Deirdre Ta.

Oliver (*setting down the tray*) Better dish these out, I suppose.

Jenny What's Mother doing?

Deirdre She's just making Father his hot milk... No, I haven't brought them.

David What?

Deirdre I didn't bring them. There wasn't room.

David But I need them badly.

Deirdre Oh, come off it, you'll survive. You managed that weekend I took them away with me by mistake.

David What was I like on the Monday though? I was fit for nothing.

Deirdre Can't say I noticed all that difference.

Oliver Do you think, just as a precaution, mind you, we ought to intercept that hot milk Mother is making for Father?

Jenny Just what I was thinking.

David Why on earth should we want to? Oh, yes, Father's hot milk, yes.

Polly Where is Father, anyway?

Deirdre Well, he stamped through the kitchen, thundered upstairs to change, crashed down again and rumbled out of the back door.

Oliver Where to?

Deirdre The shed, presumably.

Oliver What's in there?

Polly Tools.

Oliver Gardening tools? Well, I don't think we can draw any... (*He stands clicking*)

Polly Oliver. If you do that once more tonight I shall get violent.

Oliver (*irritated*) What?

Polly That damned clicking—stop it.

Jenny What's Father doing out there in the middle of the night? Does anyone know—or care?

Deirdre Well, let 'em kill themselves if they want to, I say.

Jenny Oh!

Oliver I still think we should intercept the milk.

David Hear! Hear!

Deirdre Who cares? Go on, let them kill each other off.

Jenny Will you stop saying that? It's not amusing.

Deirdre It would avoid any more dos like this one, anyway. I propose we don't intercept the milk and furthermore someone goes out in the shed and gives Father a hand to make his bomb.

David That's enough, Deirdre. This is supposedly an intelligent discussion, not a——

Deirdre Oh, bang, bang to you.

Jenny Deirdre, for heaven's sake go to bed.

Emma enters with Edward's mug of milk and a tin of biscuits

Emma There. I've made Father's milk and I've given him a call. He's pottering about out there as usual. You forgot the biscuits, Deirdre, you scatterbrain.

Oliver (*taking the mug from her*) I'll take that, Mother.

Emma Oh, all right, Oliver. Now nobody drink that by mistake, it's Father's.

Oliver puts it gingerly on the table

Edward won't touch coffee at this time of night. Hot milk with a little dash of honey, that's the only thing he'll drink. It makes him sleep like a top.

Oliver I can believe it might, yes.

Emma Now then, I haven't really forgiven you all for tonight yet. What an exhibition.

Jenny Sorry, Mother.

Emma As for you and Oliver, Polly. I've never seen such a display.

Polly Stick around.

Emma I mean, we can excuse David.

David I'm very sorry.

Emma You couldn't help being taken ill, dear.

Deirdre He's always ill, it's second nature to him. (*She sings*) It's second nature to him now…

David Oh, my God, she's off again.

Emma Just ignore her, dear, it's the only way.

David Mr Grinstead, our Sales Manager, dropped in the other day. Just for a little social chat. She stood in the hall shouting, "Grinstead, go home".

Deirdre (*singing under the following*) Polly, put the kettle on … etc.

Emma Well, she has these moods. They blow over.

David Deirdre, we're holding a conversation.

Emma (*shouting over her*) She did this as a child. Take no notice—pretend you haven't heard her.

Jenny (*shouting*) I'll throttle her in a minute.

Deirdre (*still singing*) Jenny take it off again.

David (*shouting*) Deirdre—Polly, please stop her——
Polly (*shouting*) You're being very, very boring, Deirdre.
Deirdre (*turning aggressive*) No, I'm not. I'm being very, very happy. Not a word you hear much of round here but I'm being it. Happy. Happy.
Emma That's nice, dear.
Deirdre (*picking up Father's mug*) Jolly good health to you all.
Emma (*calmly*) Don't drink that, dear, it's for your Father.
David (*half screaming*) Don't drink that, for God's sake. Stop her.

Oliver snatches the mug from Deirdre before she can drink

Deirdre What's wrong? I felt like a drop of Pa's special... (*She claps her head*) Oh. Oh my... Oh, what's happening?
Oliver Catch her, she's going.
Jenny David!

David manages to break her fall. He and Oliver drag her to the settee

David I told you. This is always happening. Imagine this in a room full of people——
Oliver Put her here. She'll be all right here.
Polly Let her sleep it off.
Jenny Quite deliberate.
Emma Smelling salts, that's what we need, smelling salts.
Jenny Mother, she doesn't need smelling salts. She's drunk.
Emma Nonsense, it's over-excitement. I've seen it before.
Jenny Deliberately drunk. She set out to ruin this evening deliberately.
Emma Now, go and get the smelling salts. They're in the kitchen.
Jenny I'm not fetching them. After all the trouble I'd gone to, to arrange this evening.
Polly Let her sleep. It's quieter.
Emma You really are heartless children.
James Shall I—get them?
Emma Oh, how kind. Thank you, James. Now, they're on the top shelf of the cupboard in the corner. If you can't reach, there's a little stepladder by the sink that I always use.
James Righto.

James exits

Emma Now stand away, David, let her get some air. (*She calls*) Can you manage, James?
James (*off*) I think so. Top shelf?

Emma (*calling*) Right at the top. In the little red tin.
James (*off*) Right.
Emma One of you girls should have gone. Really. Expecting a guest to do
  it. (*She calls*) Can you manage?
James (*off*) Yes, I'm just——

Edward enters through the other door with a hacksaw

Emma Oh, hallo, Father, been doing some woodwork?

A yell and a tremendous crash off. They look

Oliver		(*recovering*) The stepladder!
Jenny	(*together*)	Oh, no!
Polly		Oh, God!
David		I knew it!

Oliver Quickly.
Jenny Oh, no—no—no.

Oliver runs out, followed by Jenny

Edward What's that din?
Emma I think James must have had an accident.
Edward Better see if he's all right, I suppose. (*He makes for the kitchen*)
Emma (*going with him*) Those little steps never were safe, you know.
  Always a bit rickety.

Edward and Emma exit

David I can't bear to look—I just can't bear to look.
Polly He can't have fallen far.
David Father … hacksaw … steps … crash.
Deirdre Diddy sleepy now—sleepy Diddy.
Polly We'd better get your wife into bed before Mother starts giving her
  medicinal brandy for shock.
David It was bound to happen. Someone was bound to get hurt sooner or
  later—Deirdre's forgotten my pills. I have tried with her, you know, I
  really have tried. I've been patient, attentive—given her anything she
  wanted. Anything. She couldn't have had a better husband. Dry throat. (*He
  swigs Father's milk*) Come on then, I'll give you a hand.
Polly Right.
Deirdre Leggo Diddy—Diddy wants to sleepy.

As they start to lift Deirdre, David utters a startled cry and drops her

Polly What's the matter?
David (*choking, pointing at the mug*) Father's milk. I've drunk some of Father's milk.
Polly Oh. Well...
David Quickly, an emetic. Salt. Some sort of emetic.
Polly David, pull yourself together.
David Once it reaches the walls of the stomach there's nothing you can do.
Polly (*still supporting Deirdre*) David, please help me—you're perfectly all right.
David God. I think it's arsenic, I can feel my blood starting to suffocate.
Polly David, will you come and help?
David I can't move my arms.

Oliver and Edward bring on James

Edward Put him on the settee.
Oliver Right.
James (*mumbling*) I love you, Jen.
Polly (*still holding Deirdre*) What am I supposed to do with this one?
Edward Put her somewhere else. She's had her turn on here.

Jenny runs on

Jenny Why does this all have to happen today? This was going to be such a happy day.
James I love you, Jen.
Polly This is really a ludicrous family.
David (*to himself*) I'm going to sit perfectly still, slow down the pulse rate. It's the only way. Stops the blood circulating.
Oliver What's he on about?

Emma enters with a flannel

Emma I've brought a cold flannel.
David That's what they do for snake bite.
Jenny After all my careful arrangements. Why? Why?
Emma (*dabbing James's forehead; to Jenny*) Don't get excited, dear. Is that better, James?
Edward Damn dangerous those steps. Could have been you up there, Emma.
James I love you, Jen.
Emma Oh, isn't that nice?
Oliver Think we ought to summon medical help? In case of concussion, keep the patient warm and summon medical help.

Polly Thank you, Brown Owl.
Oliver Look, shut up.
David I think I'm going...
Jenny Deliberately! People have done this deliberately! I feel faint. (*She sits with her head between her knees and moans through the following*)
Oliver I don't know if I got that right about concussion.
It could be that you support the patient's head and... (*He trails off and clicks his fingers*)
Polly (*suddenly enraged*) Will you stop doing that? You are driving me mad. (*She hits Oliver on the side of his head with the biscuit tin*)
Edward Oy, oy, oy.
Emma Polly! That was a present from Auntie Susan.
Oliver Did you see that? Did you see that? She hit me. That is proof. Proof. You all saw that. I may need you to stand up in Court. My God, I think I need an Elastoplast.

Oliver stamps out

Emma Oliver!
James I love you, Jen.

Polly starts to go the other way

Edward (*to Polly*) Where are you going?
Polly For a walk. To find a steep cliff.

Polly exits

Jenny They're doing this deliberately.
Emma Jenny.
Edward Look, I can't stand any more of your din. Go upstairs if you're going to make that din.
Jenny That's right. You never liked me. Never. After all I've tried to do—you never liked me.

Jenny rushes out

Emma Oh, dear. They're all being very tiresome.
James I love you, Jen.
Emma Do you think we ought to run round and get Dr Cartwright from next door to have a look at James, dear?
Edward I'm not letting that man Cartwright in this house. He can't even behave himself in the garden. Flinging his weeds over my fence——

Act II, Scene 2

Deirdre Ma...
Emma Oh, darling.
Deirdre I don't feel very well, Ma. I think I'm going to...
Emma Oh, darling... Quickly.
Deirdre Ma——
Emma (*rushing her off*) Try and make it, dear.

Emma and Deirdre go off ⟨QC Into veano.⟩

James I love you, Jen.
Edward My God. What a household.
David Help! Help!
Edward What's the matter with you?
David Aaaaagghh! (*He points to his throat*)
Edward Something in your throat? Well, don't sit there looking useless, have a drink. (*He holds out his mug*)

James rises shakily during the following

David (*backing away*) No, no, you can't force me. I won't take it. I won't take it.

David rushes out

Edward (*turning back to James*) They're all incompatible. Every damn one of them.
James I love you, Jen... (*He collapses at the amazed Edward's feet as—*)

Black-out ⟨QC⟩

SCENE 2

The same. The next morning

Emma comes in from the kitchen to lay the breakfast

Presently, Edward enters from the front door, back from his walk

Emma Good morning, Father. Nice walk was it? Been to get the Sunday papers? Breakfast won't be long. Slept in your study last night, did you, dear? Very considerate of you, not wanting to disturb me. Oh, and thank you for switching on my electric blanket, too, dear. Only do tell me if you do that again, won't you? I slept all night without knowing it was on, you see. I don't think there's really any danger, only the man did tell us it was safer not to. After that little fire last time. One good thing, anyway, I got so hot I woke up nice and early. I'd have hated to have missed any of this gorgeous morning.

Emma goes out into the kitchen

Edward I didn't sleep a wink.
Emma (*off*) What's that, dear?
Edward I'm saying I didn't get a wink of sleep.
Emma (*off*) Yes, dear.
Edward Damn din going on all night from that spare room. Right over my head. Thumping and banging and caterwauling.

Emma enters

Emma Oh, dear. Her young man must have been having a restless night.
Edward They both were. Should have thrown a bucket of water over them.
Emma Breakfast won't be long. Anything nice to read me from the papers?

Deirdre 1 enters from upstairs

Deirdre 1 Morning, morning.
Emma Oh, good morning, darling.
Deirdre 1 Lovely day. Anyone die in the night? (*She starts downstairs*)
Emma Deirdre! What a question. Would you like cereal to start with, dear?
Deirdre 1 Jas! Come on! (*She arrives downstairs*) Morning, Pa.
Emma Or how about a nice plate of porridge?
Deirdre 1 Pa, I'm removing your uninvited guest, you'll be pleased to hear.
Emma Cereal or porridge, darling?
Deirdre 1 Yes please, Ma. Lovely. Jas!
Emma (*going out to the kitchen, confused*) Yes, dear.

Emma exits

James 1 Coming.

James 1 enters through the archway, still dressed in his shorts and laden with cases. He trips and drops them

Deirdre 1 laughs

Sorry. Morning, Mr Gray.

Edward Bloody racket.

Deirdre 1 At last. What kept you?

James 1 (*softly, to her*) Deirdre, don't you think it would be better if you stayed on a bit longer, just to see? (*He collects the cases again during the following*)

Deirdre 1 Come on, come on.

Oliver 1 enters, from the front door

Oliver 1 (*calling*) Jenny! Jenny! Anyone seen my wife? I appear to have mislaid my wife.

Deirdre 1 Jenny? Oh, that was probably her moaning in the bathroom. She's been in there all morning. No-one else has been able to get in. We're all dirty and desperate.

Oliver 1 Oh, Lord. She knows we're in a hurry. (*He calls*) Jenny! Ah, morning, Edward. What was the score at close? All out, were they?

Edward No idea.

Deirdre 1 You going past the station, Ollie?

Oliver 1 If we ever go at all, yes.

Deirdre 1 You going to give us a lift, then?

Oliver 1 Us?

Deirdre 1 Jas and me? Just to the station.

Oliver 1 I suppose so. If I must.

Deirdre 1 Ta! Come on, Jas, we've got a lift.

James 1 (*with the cases*) Deirdre, I really don't think you should leave without——

Polly 1 comes out of the bedroom

Polly 1 David! Is David there?

Oliver 1 He's out there, fiddling with that car of yours.

Polly 1 Oh, God.

Oliver 1 Oil simply pouring out of it. All over Edward's drive. (*He laughs*)

Edward glares

Polly 1 Well, tell him there's another case up here. I don't know what he's playing at. He knows we're in a hurry.

Polly 1 goes back into the bedroom

Oliver 1 Yes, so are we, Jenny!

James 1 Deirdre, I——

Deirdre 1 Dump them in Ollie's car, Jas.

Oliver 1 Yes, just dump them in Oli—(*He sees the luggage for the first time*)
You do realize, don't you, it's a car I've got, not a fork-lift truck? Hang on,
you'll need the keys. (*He fumbles in his pockets*)

An oily David 1 enters from the front door, flustered

David 1 My God! That car. That damn car!

Oliver 1 Steady there! What's your hurry?

David 1 It's not my hurry. It's Polly's hurry. I've got all the time in the world.
(*He heads towards the kitchen*) I badly need some pliers.

Deirdre 1 She says there's another case upstairs.

David 1 Who does?

Deirdre 1 Polly.

Oliver 1 finds his car keys and holds them out to James 1 impatiently

David 1 Oh, God. (*He changes direction and heads for the stairs*)

James 1 (*urgently*) Deirdre! We can't leave now. We can't.

Deirdre Oh, Jas. Stop being boring.

James 1 Doesn't anybody care what's happened? You're all just leaving.
Doesn't anybody——

His words are choked off as Oliver 1 finally puts the keys in his mouth

Oliver 1 Here.

James 1 goes reluctantly, trying to make his point through clenched teeth

Give it a half turn anti-clockwise. And mind the paintwork.

James 1 goes off through the front door

David 1 reaches the landing

David 1 Excuse me, does anyone have any pliers I could borrow by any
chance?

Nobody takes any notice

Oliver 1 (*crossing to Edward*) Goodbye, then, Edward.

Edward What?

Oliver 1 I said goodbye.

Act II, Scene 2

Edward Oh, yes. Goodbye.
Oliver 1 Try and do something about that lawn of yours sometime, will you?
Get a lot more light through these windows if you cut it now and then.
Edward Go away.
Oliver 1 Jenny! Oh, Lord.
Jenny 1 (*at the balcony, her head emerging for a second*) Coming, Oliver
dear. (*She disappears*)
David 1 Hasn't anyone got a pair of pliers?
Deirdre 1 Bye, Pa. (*She calls to the kitchen*) Ma! Goodbye!

Emma enters from the kitchen

Emma Oh, Deirdre, darling. Did you say you wanted cereal or porridge?
Deirdre 1 Sorry, Ma. We have to run.
Emma What about your breakfast?
Deirdre 1 Byeee!

Deirdre 1 goes out the front door

Deidre (Penny)
Back into crumpled
evening dress

Emma I haven't got your new address.
David 1 Pliers.
Emma Oh, good morning, David.
Oliver 1 Oh, Mother. 'Fraid you'll have to scrub round that porridge of mine
as well ... we must dash.
David 1 It's an emergency.
Oliver 1 (*going off angrily*) You're damn right it is. We're an hour late
already. Jenny!

Oliver 1 goes off

Emma You and Polly are stopping for breakfast, aren't you, David? Cereal
or porridge?
David 1 I just want pliers, that's all.
Emma Right. I'll make you some in just a second, David. (*She starts after
Deirdre 1*) Deirdre, darling, your address.

Emma goes out the front door

David 1 (*weakly*) Oh, God. Pliers... pliers... (*He appeals to heaven*)
Edward (*quietly*) In the shed.
David 1 (*startled*) What?
Edward Pliers. In the shed.
David 1 (*brightening*) Oh, really?

Edward Right hand shelf. In the box.
David 1 (*eternally grateful*) Oh, thank you. Thank you very much, Father.

Polly 1 appears with a suitcase

Polly 1 David! Case!
David 1 Just a moment, dear.
Polly 1 I do have a meeting, you know.

Polly 1 exits

David 1 exits

Emma enters

Emma (*to herself*) Now, let's see. How many of them want breakfast now? That's——
Edward (*yelling after David 1*) And put them back when you've finished with them.
Emma Yes, dear. That's two, three ... four, who don't want anything to eat at all and...
Edward And one who does.
Emma Who's that, dear?
Edward Me.
Emma Oh, yes. Well, I'm not counting you at the moment, dear.

James 2 comes downstairs

James 2 Morning, sir. Morning, Mrs Gray.

Edward stares at him, somewhat baffled

Emma Oh, good morning, James. Did you sleep well? Polly's not down yet, I don't think.
James 2 No. Well, actually, I wondered if it would be all right if I took Polly up something on a tray, Mrs Gray.
Emma Oh. What exactly did you want to take up, dear?
James 2 Food. Breakfast.
Emma Oh. Oh, I see. How very sweet of you. Wake her up with a nice surprise. She'll appreciate that. Cereal or porridge?
James 2 Just some toast, Mrs Gray. That's what she always has, anyway ... so I'm given to understand... I'd hazard a guess at that, anyway...
Emma Toast. Right.

James 2 (*moving to the kitchen door*) No. I'll do it, Mrs Gray. I'll do it. Don't worry. (*He tries again with Edward*) Good morning, sir.
Edward Good morning.

James 2 exits to the kitchen

Edward Who the hell was that?
Emma Polly's James, dear.
Edward (*mystified*) Polly's James?
Emma (*calling*) Oh, James, there are some boiled eggs out there if you'd like to... Oh, my goodness. Those eggs! They'll be completely hard-boiled.
Edward Well, give them to them in a bag. They can eat them on the way.
Emma (*going*) What a good idea.
Edward I wasn't serious, woman. They don't want to be loaded down with hard-boiled eggs, do they?

Emma goes out to the kitchen

Oliver 1 enters

Oliver 1 (*calling*) Jenny! Would you please come along?
Jenny 1 (*off*) Coming, dear.

Jenny 1 enters at the top of the stairs

Oliver 1 (*seeing Edward*) Now then, Edward. Going to behave yourself if we leave you on your own, are you? (*He laughs nervously*)
Edward What do you mean by that?
Oliver 1 Nothing. Nothing at all.

Jenny 1 reaches the bottom of the stairs

Jenny, what on earth do you find to do in the bathroom all this time? Do you clean each of your teeth individually or what?
Jenny 1 (*very queasy*) Sorry, dear.
Oliver 1 It's hardly fair to inflict our children on Mrs Curtis all day Sunday, Jenny.
Jenny 1 (*in a low voice*) Oliver, I'm desperately worried about leaving Mother and Father on their own.
Oliver 1 (*with a glance at Edward*) Yes, well, it's not an ideal arrangement but there's nothing much we can do about it, is there?
Jenny 1 Is Deirdre staying or not?
Oliver 1 Not. She's coming with us, she's in the car—waiting—as we all are.

Jenny 1 Oh well, that's it then, that settles it. I'll phone Mrs Curtis and ask her to look after you and the children, just for a few days.

Oliver 1 Wonderful. Wonderful.

Jenny 1 I'm sure she wouldn't mind.

Oliver 1 Jenny, if you're proposing that I divorce you and set up house with Mrs Curtis...

Jenny 1 Oh, God——

Oliver 1 I'll give it serious consideration but...

Jenny 1 All right. All right. Forget it. Forget I spoke. On your head be it. (*Shrilly*) On your head be it.

Edward (*looking up*) Eh?

Jenny 1 (*immediately soothing*) Nothing, Father, nothing. I'll say goodbye to Mother. (*She mouths to Oliver 1*) On your head be it.

Jenny 1 goes off into the kitchen

Oliver 1 Oh dear, oh dear. Mind if I take a look at the business section? (*He plucks the paper from Edward's hands*) Thank you.

James 1 enters from the front door

James 1 Deirdre's forgotten her handbag.

Oliver 1 (*furiously*) Oh, no. I can see I'm going to spend my Sunday sitting in the drive.

Oliver 1 goes out the front door

James 1 (*calling after him*) Won't be a second. (*He starts his search*)

Emma enters from the kitchen, followed by Jenny 1

Emma (*calling behind her as she comes in*) I should turn the grill down a little next time, James. It always was a bit fierce.

Jenny 1 Mother, are you sure you'll be...?

Emma Of course I'm sure, dear. Now what was I looking for? Salt.

Jenny 1 I was just talking to Oliver, Mother, and he said——

Emma Hallo, Jas dear. Are you all right?

James 1 (*lying on the floor peering under an armchair*) Handbag, Deirdre's handbag, Mrs Gray. (*He continues to search, moving towards Edward*)

Emma Oh, I see.

Jenny 1 Mother, it would be quite easy for me to arrange for Mrs Curtis to look after the children...

David 1 enters from the front door, agitated

David 1 Rag. I need a piece of rag.
Emma What for, dear?
David 1 Just a spot of oil on the drive, I'm afraid.
Emma (*going out*) Well, come in here, David, I'll give you one.

Emma goes out into the kitchen

David 1 (*following her*) Thank you. (*Anxiously to Edward*) It's only a drop.

David 1 goes out into the kitchen

Jenny 1 moves towards Edward but James 1 is now by his chair

Edward What the devil are you up to?
James 1 Er ... handbag. Deirdre's handbag.
Edward Well, I haven't got it. Look upstairs.
James 1 Upstairs?
Edward You don't know much about women's handbags, do you?
James 1 Er...
Edward If you're downstairs, they're upstairs, if you're upstairs, they're
bound to be downstairs.
James 1 Ah. Upstairs. Yes. (*He crosses to the stairs. To Jenny 1*) Sorry to
keep you and Oliver waiting. Deirdre's handbag. Upstairs.
Jenny 1 Quite all right.

James 1 bounds upstairs

Jenny 1 moves to Edward

David 1 enters with a cloth from the kitchen

David 1 Got one.
Edward Good for you.
David 1 (*hurrying out*) Only a spot. Mop it up in no time.

David 1 goes out

Jenny 1 Goodbye, Father. I hope everything will be all right.
Edward So do I.
Jenny 1 Goodbye, then.
Edward Goodbye.
Jenny 1 Goodbye. (*Loathing to leave him, she crosses to the front door*) Bye.

Edward reacts with annoyance

Polly 1 appears at the top of the stairs

Polly 1 (*calling*) David! (*She starts downstairs*)

James 1, clutching a handbag, comes rushing down ahead of her

James 1 (*to Edward*) Got it. Thank you, sir.

James 1 goes out the front door

Emma enters from the kitchen with fruit juice and bags of eggs

Polly 1 (*still on her way down, calling*) David!
Emma Here we are, Edward. Some fruit juice to be getting on with. Where on earth is Jenny?
Edward I'm not drinking this neat. Burns my stomach, you know that. I'll wait for my porridge. Hopefully...
Polly 1 (*at the bottom of the stairs*) David!
Emma It's coming in a minute, dear.
Polly 1 Have you seen David, Mother?
Edward He's busy flooding my drive with car oil.
Polly 1 He knows I've got a meeting to go to.
Emma Oh dear, another one?
Polly 1 Yes, Mother.
Emma Porridge or cereal, dear?
Polly 1 I'll just help myself, Mother. (*She makes for the kitchen*)
Emma I mean, if you spent a little more time at home with David, you might find... (*tailing off*) you had a little more in common.

Polly 1 exits

James 1 enters from the front door with the handbag

James 1 (*to Edward*) Wrong one, sir.
Emma (*seeing him*) Oh. Jas, dear. Is that my handbag?
James 1 Oh. I'm terribly sorry, Mrs Gray, I... (*He gives her the bag*)

James 1 hurries upstairs

Emma How extraordinary.
Edward Check your purse.
Emma Why?
Edward Fellow's desperate to buy himself some trousers.

Polly 1 enters from the kitchen with coffee and a bowl of cereal

Polly 1 Well, I'll collect David and be off. Goodbye, Father.
Emma Is that enough for you, dear?
Polly 1 Ample, Mother.
Emma No, I was saying, dear, if you and David could find some sort of mutual hobby…
Polly 1 Good idea, Mother.
Emma Colonel and Mrs Wilkins in the village, you know, they very nearly separated. At their age. Then they both bought bicycles each and they've been everywhere together. Last summer they went all the way to Truro.
Polly 1 (*kissing her casually*) Goodbye, Mother.
Emma Not that I'm suggesting that you and David take up cycling.
Polly 1 Look, I'm going now. Can I safely leave you two together?
Edward Eh?
Emma Just some little mutual hobby, dear.
Polly 1 Well, try and behave like grown up people, won't you?
Emma Here you are. (*She hands Polly 1 a bag*)
Polly 1 What's this?
Emma Hard-boiled eggs, dear, for the journey.
Polly 1 Oh. Thank you very much. I'm sure they'll come in handy. Bye. Goodbye, Father. Take good care of Mother, won't you?
Edward Good luck with the bicycle.
Polly 1 I'll send you a card from Truro.

Polly 1 goes out the front door

Emma Just some little mutual hobby, dear. (*She gives up*) Now, let's see, how many cereals and how many porridges is it now…
Edward (*in his newspaper*) There's a chap here has spent three years building a model of the QE2 out of old corned beef tins.
Emma Really? How very clever of him.
Edward Bloody waste of time if you ask me. I suppose there's no chance of my getting anything to eat?

Deirdre 3 appears at the top of the stairs, supported by David 3. She is still in her evening dress, now very crumpled, wears dark glasses, and looks very hung over

David 3 (*easing her along*) Easy … easy … easy, now.
Deirdre 3 Don't shout. Whatever you do, don't shout.
Emma Good gracious, Deirdre dear. Are you all right?
David 3 She's just a little fragile.

Emma Would you like some cereal, darling, or some nice porridge, perhaps?
Deirdre 3 Ugh!
David 3 No, I don't think she would, Mother.

Deirdre 3 and David 3 start slowly downstairs

Edward Emma … while you're on the subject of porridge—since I'm the
only person in this house who appears to want any, could you explain to
me why I'm also the only one who's unable to get any? Is there some damn
conspiracy to starve me to death?

*Deirdre 3 and David 3 reach the bottom of the stairs. Emma concentrates on
them*

David 3 Death, death? Who said death?
Emma I should fetch her coat, David. She looks very chilly. You really must
learn to look after her.
David 3 Are you sure you'll be all right on your own, Mother?
Emma Of course I will, dear. Don't worry about me. Worry about your wife.
David 3 I do. Continually. I've got ulcers worrying about her.
Edward All she needs is a run round the garden and a good dose of salts.
Emma Salt. (*She dashes back to the table to fetch a paper bag*) Here we are.
Boiled eggs. For the journey.

Deirdre 3 reacts

David 3 Thank you, Mother. Take care … take care.
Emma Get her into the air, David. She needs air.
David 3 Yes, goodbye. Goodbye, Father.

David 3 and Deirdre 3 go out the front door

Emma She really does look very peaky. I don't think David looks after her
at all well.

Polly 2 appears in the archway in pyjamas

Polly 2 James…
Emma Oh, good morning, Polly dear. Sleep well?
Polly 2 Oh, Mother, James and I are staying on till this evening.
Emma Oh.
Polly 2 Just for a talk.
Emma How nice.

Polly 2 Yes, isn't it, Mother? Oh—and tell James it doesn't take an hour and a half to make a piece of toast.
Emma He may be having trouble with that grill, dear.
Polly 2 Well, tell him to hurry up and come back to bed. I'm cold.

Polly 2 exits

Emma It's odd, you know, Edward. Ever since you kindly fixed that grill for me—if you turn it on full, the flames shoot straight out into your face.
Edward Better learn to duck.
Emma I have, dear, don't worry.

James 3 comes downstairs

James 3 Mrs Gray.
Emma Oh, good morning, Jimmy. Did you sleep well?
James 3 Mrs Gray. I have to stay on.
Emma Oh, good.
James 3 I have to stand by Jenny.
Emma That's nice.
James 3 She needs me. She may not know she needs me but she does.
Emma I'm sure she does. What would you like for breakfast, Jimmy?
James 3 I'm not leaving this house while I'm needed. Good morning, Mr Gray.
Edward Good morning, whoever you are.
James 3 Jimmy. I'm Jimmy. Remember?
Emma Jenny's Jimmy, dear.
Edward (*baffled*) Jenny's Jimmy?
Emma Cereal or porridge?

Jenny 3 comes downstairs with James 3's suitcase

Jenny 3 Jimmy! Jimmy!
Emma Good morning, Jenny. Sleep well?
Jenny 3 Morning, Mother. You forgot your suitcase, Jimmy. You'll be needing it.
Emma Not during breakfast, dear.
Jenny 3 (*holding out the case to James 3*) Here. Take it.
James 3 I'm staying by you, Jen.
Emma Jimmy was just saying how much you need him just at the moment, Jenny.
Jenny 3 I don't need him. I don't need anyone.
James 3 I'm staying.

Jenny 3 I'm capable of coping with this alone. I'm sorry but my own flesh
and blood has to come first, Jimmy.
Emma You mean the baby, dear?
Jenny 3 No, I'm not talking about the baby, Mother. (*To James 3*) Go
away.
James 3 Jen, you can't cope with all this alone.
Jenny 3 Go away. Before it's too late. And never come back.

Jenny 3 dashes out into the kitchen

Edward They'll put her away for good one of these days.
Emma Jimmy...
James 3 It's not fair. I've never felt more needed in my life—I need to be
needed—and she doesn't need me.

James 3 rushes out the front door

Emma Oh, dear. (*She pauses*) We're going to have an awful lot of porridge
left over at this rate. I made masses.

Oliver 2 appears upstairs

Oliver 2 Well, surely we have time for a coffee, Deirdre.
Edward I suppose from having none at all, I'm going to be up to my neck
in the stuff.

Oliver 2 comes downstairs

Emma Oh, good morning, Oliver. Little Deirdre up yet?
Oliver 2 Still putting on a second coat of paint, I think. Morning, Edward...
(*He sees the table*) Oh. When he got there, the cupboard was bare... Any
breakfast going, Emma?
Emma Breakfast? Oh, yes, dear. Cereal or porridge?
Oliver 2 Well, I think I could probably squeeze in a bit of each, actually,
Emma.
Emma Oh, that's splendid. Sit down. I'll bring it out.
Oliver 2 Won't take too long will it, Emma? Only as soon as Deirdre gets
down we've got to be off. She's giving some idiotic luncheon party.
Emma Oh, that's nice. Who's coming? Anyone I know?
Oliver 2 Shouldn't think so. Shouldn't think it's anyone I know, either. She
just leans out of the window and invites people. Three total strangers and
no food in the house. Should be a riot.
Emma Lovely, dear.

Emma goes out to the kitchen

Oliver 2 crosses to Edward

Oliver 2 I say, Edward...
Edward Eh?
Oliver 2 Just occurred to me—you wouldn't care to come and have lunch at our place, would you? Leave the old lady behind for once. Have a bit of a chat. Do you good. Change of air.
Edward I'm perfectly happy with the air I've got, thank you. Once was quite enough.
Oliver 2 Oh, well. Just a thought.

James 2 enters from the kitchen—with Polly 2's breakfast tray. Two pieces of toast, a small pot of coffee, etc.

James 2 Hallo.
Oliver 2 Hallo. There's a chap who's got himself organised. Breakfast cafeteria style, eh?
James 2 No, I'm just taking this up to Polly in bed.
Oliver 2 Oh, well. Keep at it. (*He laughs*)

James 2 smiles weakly

Don't forget to take her order for lunch, will you?
James 2 (*defiantly*) No. I won't.
Oliver 2 I say, that's interesting. Did you know you had no eyelashes?
James 2 Yes.
Oliver 2 What is it? Hereditary—run in the family, does it?
James 2 No, it's that gas stove out there. The flame shot out when I lit it.
Oliver 2 Ah. Act of God, eh? I see. Well, if you do get fed up with providing meals on wheels for Polly, you could always come over and have lunch at our place with Deirdre's friends. He'd enjoy that, wouldn't he, Edward?
Edward Eh?
Oliver 2 He came to dinner with us once, didn't you, Edward? That was enough for him. Deirdre got him tiddly. He finished up falling in the swimming pool.
Edward Nonsense. Somebody pushed me. Damn lucky I didn't sue you.
Oliver 2 Oh, come on, Edward, the only person who could have pushed you was... (*He hastily returns his attention to James 2*) Well? What about it? Lunch? Might be your last chance to get away.
James 2 Yes. Well, I'll think about it.
Oliver 2 You do that. You do that. Polly's got whole cupboards filled with chaps like you.

James 2 Nonsense.
Oliver 2 Dozens of them, hanging up in rows. She's particularly fond of them between two slices of—ah, I see you've already made some... (*He laughs*)

James 2 goes out

Ah, is that fruit juice you've got there, Edward?
Edward What? Oh, yes, fruit juice. Yes.
Oliver 2 Where did that originate? Any idea?
Edward I don't know. The kitchen, presumably.
Oliver 2 Might as well fill up while I'm here. Have you finished with the colour supplement by any chance, Edward? (*He takes it*) Thanks.

Oliver 2 goes out into the kitchen

David 1 comes in the front door

David 1 Is Polly down yet?
Edward Possibly.
David 1 It's not my day, it really isn't. First Polly, then the car... Oh, I put the pliers back. And the first aid tin...
Edward What about it?
David 1 I didn't touch it. Father ... if you're—planning to do—something else... Whatever it is—you're planning to do... If you are that is... Please don't. I couldn't bear it. I couldn't.
Edward (*confidentially*) I'll let you in on a secret, shall I?
David 1 Oh? What's that?
Edward In a moment, I am about to become—extremely violent.
David 1 Oh no, no...
Edward And do you know why I'm going to become violent? Because I have been sitting here most of the morning listening to gibbering lunatics like yourself, and during the whole of that time I have not had a single bite to eat. Would someone be kind enough to tell me— (*he rises to a crescendo*) why I cannot get a simple plate of *porridge! Emma!*

David 1 flees through the front door

The kitchen door flies open and Emma hurries in with Jenny 3 behind her

James 2 enters from upstairs

Emma Edward, dear, what is it?
Edward I am hungry, Emma. Hungry. I am not a man to be trifled with when I'm hungry.

Emma It's coming, dear, it's just coming. Jenny, dear. Father's porridge.
Jenny 3 (*going to the kitchen*) Yes, Mother.

Jenny 3 exits

Emma It's coming, dear. Hallo, James. All right?
James 2 Yes, thank you. Oliver hasn't gone, has he, Mr Gray?
Edward Possibly.
Emma He's in the kitchen, dear.
James 2 Oh, right. Thank you. (*He starts downstairs*)

Jenny 3 enters from the kitchen with a plate of porridge

Jenny 3 Here you are, Father. Your porridge. Be careful, it's very hot.

Deirdre 2 appears at the top of the stairs

James 2 goes off to the kitchen

Deirdre 2 Well, here I am at last. As large as life and twice as lovely.
Emma Good morning, Deirdre, darling.

Deirdre 2 comes downstairs

Deirdre 2 Where's Ollie?
Emma (*giving her a kiss*) You do look nice, what a lovely scent. Oh, I think
he's in the kitchen, dear.
Deirdre 2 I thought he was ready to go.

Edward tastes his porridge and splutters

Edward Emma... Is this your concoction?
Emma Yes, dear.
Edward Tastes like old gum boots.
Jenny 3 Oh.
Deirdre 2 (*calling*) Ollie! We're going! Morning, Pa.
Edward You going, are you?

As they talk, Jenny 3 surreptitiously creeps up on Edward's porridge

Deirdre 2 'Fraid so, Pa.
Edward Taking the rest of my flowers with you, are you?
Deirdre 2 Oh, thank you, Pa.

Edward Help yourself. There's a hedge out there if you fancy it.

Deirdre 2 exits into the kitchen

Just uproot it as you go.

Jenny 3 sticks her finger into Edward's porridge and samples it cautiously

(*Roaring*) Get your filthy hands out of my food, girl!
Jenny 3 Sorry, Father.
Emma Jenny, really.

Jenny 3 hurries into the kitchen

Edward What's that mucky little beast playing at?
Emma I'm sure I don't know. I can't think where she picked up habits like
that from.

Polly 3 comes downstairs

Polly 3 Morning, Father.
Emma Ah, Polly. Sleep well?
Polly 3 Mother.
Emma Now, I hope you've got over that nasty little mood of yours, Polly.
Polly 3 Mood? What mood's that, Mother?
Emma I hope you've made things up with Oliver, that's all. I've never seen
such behaviour.

Oliver 3 comes downstairs

Oliver 3 Morning, Emma. Morning, Edward.
Emma (*giving him a kiss*) Good morning, Oliver.
Edward Morning.
Emma Polly's here waiting for you, Oliver.
Oliver 3 Good heavens, so she is. That's made my day, that has.
Polly 3 Enjoy it. It could be your last.
Oliver 3 Ah. Is that porridge you're eating, Edward? Looks very nice.
Polly 3 You haven't time for that.
Emma Would you care for some before you go, Oliver?
Oliver 3 Wouldn't say no, Emma.
Polly 3 You haven't time.
Emma It won't take me a moment.
Polly 3 No, Mother, he hasn't time.

Oliver 3 What do you mean, I haven't time. I've got all day.

Polly 3 If you think you can wake me up at the crack of dawn bellowing and shouting that you're in a hurry to get back...

Oliver 3 Bellowing and shouting?

Polly 3 And then expect me to sit here...

Oliver 3 What's the woman talking about? When did I bellow and shout?

Polly 3 While you gorge your way through porridge...

Oliver 3 She even begrudges me food.

Emma You mustn't begrudge him food, Polly.

Polly 3 I begrudge him one hell of a lot besides food. He expects the bloody world served up to him on a plate.

Emma Polly!

Polly 3 No, Mother. To hell with him.

Oliver 3 Oh, go on, clear off, you stupid bitch.

Emma Oliver!

Edward There's something very odd about this fruit juice.

A pause

Emma Oh, dear.

Oliver 3 Don't drink it, Father. I wouldn't drink it.

Edward Tastes decidedly odd.

Polly 3 It does?

Edward (*handing the glass to Emma*) Have a taste of that. See what you think.

Emma (*sniffing it*) Oh.

Polly 3 No, Mother, don't touch it. It might be off. Let Oliver try it. (*She thrusts the glass into Oliver 3's hand*)

Oliver 3 (*giving it back*) Me? I'm not trying it. You try it yourself.

Emma Don't let's quarrel. I'll throw it away and open a fresh carton. That's the best thing.

Polly 3 (*keeping hold of the glass*) I'll take it, Mother. You stay here.

Emma Oh, thank you, dear.

Polly 3 goes off into the kitchen with the glass

Edward Probably Jenny's been at it. Washing her feet in it or something.

Jenny 2 comes out of the bedroom

Jenny 2 Wait there, David darling. Just wait there.

Emma Good morning, Jenny dear.

Jenny 2 closes the bedroom door and hurries down the stairs

Oliver 3 What was the score at close, Edward? All out, were they?
Edward Couldn't give a damn.
Oliver 3 Mind if I take a look? (*He takes the main section of the paper and sits on the sofa*)
Jenny 2 (*hurrying towards the kitchen*) Good morning.
Emma Hallo, dear ... are you...?
Jenny 2 Must just get a glass of water, Mother. Won't be a minute.
Emma Oh, dear, you're not...?
Jenny 2 No, it's David. He's feverish. He was terribly restless last night.
Emma There's water upstairs.
Jenny 2 No, he won't drink upstairs water in case the tank's infected. He'll only drink it straight from the rising main.
Edward If he knew where that came from he wouldn't drink that either.
Jenny 2 Oh, for heaven's sake, don't tell him that.

Jenny 2 goes into the kitchen. She passes Polly 3 coming back with fruit juice

Polly 3 Try this. Here. (*She gives Edward the drink*)
Edward Looks a bit cloudy.
Polly 3 Probably. I spat in it.
Edward Don't be disgusting.
Polly 3 Coming?
Oliver 3 Whenever you're ready, darling.
Polly 3 Goodbye, Mother.
Emma Goodbye, dear. Now do try, won't you?
Polly 3 Father...
Edward Mmmm?
Polly 3 We're going. Goodbye.
Edward Oh, goodbye then.
Oliver 3 (*moving off to the front door*) Bye.
Polly 3 Give me the keys, Oliver. I'm driving.
Oliver 3 (*going out of the front door, still with Edward's paper*) Oh no, you're not. Not on the motorway.
Polly 3 (*following him*) Oliver, will you kindly give me the keys...?
Oliver 3 I'm sorry, I have no intention of travelling with you again on the motorway.
Polly 3 Oliver! Oliver!

Oliver 3 and Polly 3 are gone

Edward Hey! My paper!

Jenny 2 enters with a glass of water from the kitchen

Jenny 2 Just give him this. He can't swallow them without water.
Emma There's some aspirin in the bathroom cabinet if you need them, dear.
Jenny 2 That's all right, Mother. David has his own pills.

An ashen David 2 appears at the bedroom door

David 2 (*feebly*) Jenny...
Jenny 2 (*starting towards him*) Darling! What are you doing standing up?

David 2 begins to sway about alarmingly

(*Running upstairs to him*) Coming, darling, coming. Oh, darling. (*She reaches David 2 and steadies him*)
Edward Worst possible choice she could have made.

During the next section Jenny 2 guides David 2 slowly down the stairs

Deirdre 2 enters from the kitchen

Deirdre 2 That hog of a husband of mine has eaten four boiled eggs. A plate of cereal, a plate of porridge and four hard boiled tepid eggs.
Emma It's nice to see a man with an appetite, dear.
Deirdre 2 I think it's disgusting. (*She calls*) Ollie! God, I think he's still at it. Ollie!

Oliver 2 enters from the kitchen, pleased with himself

Oliver 2 Coming. All set, are we?
Deirdre 2 We are departing, Mother.
Emma Right, dear.

Jenny 2 and David 2 reach the bottom of the stairs. David 2 groans

Emma (*hurrying to them*) Oh, poor David. How are you feeling?
Oliver 2 Good grief. Here he comes. The out-patient of the year.
Jenny 2 He'd be better off at home, Mother. He always calms down at home.
David 2 Get home. Just get home.
Edward Do you think he'll make it that far?
Jenny 2 Father!

Jenny 2 and Emma sit David 2 down

David 2 I'm so dry. I'm completely dried out.

Emma Well, have a little drink, dear. Here... (*She takes up Edward's fruit juice and starts to feed it to David 2*)

Jenny 2 (*quietly*) I must get him away. I must get him away from this house.

Emma Is that better, David?

David 2 (*faintly*) A little.

Jenny 2 Is Polly staying on?

James 2 Yes. Just Polly.

Jenny 2 Oh, that's wonderful. That's a weight off my mind.

Emma I think David could do with a little holiday, don't you, Edward? Perhaps he could come and stay here.

Jenny 2 Oh no, Mother.

Oliver 2 I say, before you make any definite plans for him—is your husband still breathing?

Jenny 2 (*rushing to David 2*) What? (*She slaps his face*)

He revives

Yes, yes. Of course he is. Here, darling. (*She takes the fruit juice from Emma and continues to feed David*)

Deirdre 2 (*impatiently*) Ollie.

Oliver 2 Oh, yes, yes. We must be off, Emma. Thanks for the snackerette. You cook a good egg. Bit on the hard-boiled side but ... that fruit juice seemed a bit odd, though.

Emma Oh, dear. Did you drink some of Father's juice? I don't think you should have.

Oliver 2 Why not?

Emma Well, Father seemed to think there was something rather peculiar about it.

Oliver 2 Eh?

Edward Damn woman had been messing around with it out there.

Jenny 2 freezes with horror

Jenny 2 Oh.

Oliver 2 (*equally appalled*) Oh—really?

Jenny 2 (*snatching the glass from David 2*) David—don't drink it!

Oliver 2 Father's fruit juice.

David 2 Father's fruit juice! Oh, my God. (*He rises in horror*)

Deirdre 2 You coming, Ollie?

David 2 Get me out.

Oliver 2 Yes ... yes... (*He loosens his collar*)

David 2 Get me out of here.

Deirdre 2 What's the matter with you?

Oliver 2 Nothing ... nothing at all ... tell you later.

Emma Is anything wrong?

David 2 I can't move my legs.
Jenny 2 (*helping him to the door*) Quickly, darling.
Oliver 2 Bye.
Deirdre 2 Bye, Ma. Bye, Pa.
David 2 I must get out.
Jenny 2 Yes, dear.
James 2 (*appearing on the landing*) Oliver.
Emma What on earth's the matter with you all?
David 2 Get me out of this house.
Jenny 2 Goodbye, Mother.
Emma (*following them all*) You really are the most extraordinary children at times.

As Emma, Oliver 2, Deirdre 2, David 2, and Jenny 2 go out of the front door, James 2 hurries downstairs

James 2 (*darting past Emma*) Oliver… Wait for me.

James 2 rushes out of the front door

The bedroom door upstairs slams open. Polly's voice is heard

Polly 2 (*off*) James! James! Where the hell have you got to?

Polly 2 comes out of the bedroom

What was all that row? (*She starts downstairs*)
Edward It's getting increasingly difficult to read a paper in this house.
Polly 2 Hallo, Father.
Edward How long are you thinking of staying?
Polly 2 Just for a bit.
Edward Pleased to hear it.
Polly 2 Thank you, Father.
Edward Well, now you've condescended to get out of bed, you can make me some toast.
Polly 2 My pleasure. I know just the man to make it. If you don't mind waiting… (*She calls*) James! You haven't seen him, have you?
Edward Possibly.

Polly 2 moves to the kitchen door

Polly 2 James!

Emma enters through the front door

Emma James has just left, dear, didn't you know?
Polly 2 What do you mean, left?
Emma I've just waved them all off. Oliver invited him to lunch.
Polly 2 Oliver?
Emma Yes, he went off in the car with him and Deirdre.
Polly 2 Oh. I see.
Emma (*going upstairs*) Didn't he tell you?
Polly 2 Of course he did.
Emma Let's see if there's anyone left up here who'd like breakfast.

Emma exits upstairs

Polly looks annoyed

Edward Escaped from the cupboard, has he?
Polly 2 Sorry?
Edward Your chap? Fallen off his coat hanger?
Polly 2 I think you're finally going senile, Father. I have to say it.
Edward If you want to keep a man you'd better learn how to hang him up properly.

Polly 2 exits and slams the kitchen door

Deirdre 1 comes in the front door

Deirdre 1 (*calling*) Jas! Pa, have you seen Jas?
Edward Who?
Deirdre 1 My young gentleman, Pa. Have you seen him? (*She calls upstairs*) Jas! He came in to get my handbag ages ago. I've been sitting in the car with Ollie watching him turn puce. (*She calls*) Jas!

James 1 appears at the archway

James 1 (*holding up the bag*) Is this it?
Deirdre 1 What happened to you? Ollie's hopping mad out there.
James 1 Had a job finding it. It was under the bed.
Deirdre 1 First place I always look for anything. Shouldn't have taken you that long.
James 1 (*softly*) Not your bed ... my bed.
Deirdre 1 That's what fell off in the night.

Deirdre 1 giggles, sees Edward glowering at her and checks herself. James 1 comes downstairs

James 1 Deirdre, don't you think that you really ought to stay on?
Deirdre 1 Come on.
James 1 Where are you going to stay when you get back to London?
Deirdre 1 Where else?
James 1 My place, you mean?
Deirdre 1 You're not shocked or something?
James 1 No, no. It's not that. Oughtn't you to stay here?
Deirdre 1 You owe me a flat. We can get thrown out of yours tonight.
James 1 OK, then. If you don't mind sharing a room.
Deirdre 1 Why else would I come?
James 1 With my aunt.
Deirdre 1 Your aunt? You sleep with your aunt?
James 1 No, she's in the other room. Uncle's in with me. They're not on
speaking terms at present.
Deirdre 1 I thought you said you had a flat on your own?
James 1 I do. They're only there temporarily.
Deirdre 1 Well, how long's temporarily?
James 1 Just till my grandmother's better.
Deirdre 1 Grandmother?
James 1 She sleeps in the sitting room. Till her leg's out of plaster, anyway.
We could probably squeeze you in, though——
Deirdre 1 Thanks.

Oliver 1 comes in the front door

Oliver 1 (*furiously*) Now listen to me, you two. I have been sitting out in that
drive in my car for twenty minutes with the engine running. If you're not
out there in ten seconds, I'm unloading your luggage and leaving without
you. Is that clear?
Deirdre 1 I think you'd better do just that, Ollie.
Oliver 1 What did you say?
Deirdre 1 Would you unload my luggage again, please?
Oliver 1 Unload it? Did you say unload it?
Deirdre 1 Yes. Unfortunately, certain arrangements have fallen through so
I'm having to stay on.
Oliver 1 My God. Twenty minutes. Twenty minutes. (*To James 1*) Am I to
take it you're staying as well?
Deirdre 1 No. Just me.
Oliver 1 Fine. Fine. Just as long as I know. Perhaps you'd care to give me
a hand to unload it. It took me ten minutes to get it all in in the first place,
but never mind.

Deirdre 1 goes out to the front door

James 1 I'm terribly sorry.
Oliver 1 Here. (*He hands a pair of old, rolled up trousers to James 1*)
James 1 What's this?
Oliver 1 (*irritably*) Trousers. Weren't you asking me for trousers?
James 1 Oh. Well, I don't really need them now.

Oliver 1 snatches them back from him and storms out

Er—goodbye, sir.
Edward Goodbye. And my warmest regards to your grandmother.
James 1 Oh. Thank you.
Edward Wherever she may be.
James 1 Goodbye.
Edward Better luck next time.

James 1 goes out

Emma enters from upstairs

Emma No. Nobody left up there at all. I don't know what we're going to do with all that porridge.

Polly 2 enters from the kitchen with Edward's toast

Polly 2 Here you are, Father.
Emma Ah, Polly.
Polly 2 I hope you like it well done.
Emma Good Lord. What peculiar-looking toast.
Polly 2 Best I could do, Mother.
Emma It'll be lovely having you here for a little, Polly.
Polly 2 Yes, it's only for a little, Mother. Just till we get things straight. (*She sits on the sofa*)

Jenny 3 enters from the kitchen. She wears an apron and rubber gloves

Jenny 3 Now then, Mother.
Emma Oh, Jenny. You look busy.
Jenny 3 I've just been giving everything a bit of a wipe over out there. Nothing drastic. Am I the only one left?
Emma Yes, the only one. You'll be staying a little while you say, dear?
Jenny 3 Just for a while, Mother. (*She sits next to Polly 2*)
Emma That's nice.

Deirdre 1 enters from the front door with a couple of cases

Deirdre 1 Hell! Hallo, Ma.

Emma Deirdre! I thought you'd gone.

Deirdre 1 No. Well, actually, Ma, there's been a slight change of plan. (*She throws herself down beside Polly 2 and Jenny 3*)

Emma You'll be staying for a little, I hope?

Deirdre 1 Er ... just a day or so, Mother.

Emma Oh, that's wonderful.

Deirdre 1 Yes, I thought you'd be pleased.

Emma Is—er... Jas staying too?

Deirdre 1 No. He's not. I was rather elaborately ditched.

Emma Oh yes, dear. I thought he was a very lively young man. Didn't you think so, Edward?

Edward Who?

Emma Deirdre's Jas, dear.

Edward The one in the shorts, you mean? Oh yes, he was lively all right.

Emma Just one word of warning about him, Polly, dear. He could be just the tiniest bit dishonest. Did you know that, Edward?

Edward Who?

Emma Polly's James, dear. Do listen.

Edward Oh him, yes.

Emma I caught him trying to steal all my little cakes, of all things. He had Jenny's knitting bag full of them.

Polly 2 Just shows how popular they are, Mother.

Emma All the same, I think you've got a real treasure there, Jenny. I mean, there are not many young men who'd...

Jenny 3 No, Mother. I'm sure there aren't.

Emma Jenny's very lucky to have someone prepared to stand by her. Isn't she, Edward?

Edward Who?

Emma Jenny's Jimmy, dear.

Edward Oh, yes. Great stroke of good fortune.

Emma Now, dear. I've been wanting to say this to you all weekend. And at last I've got you on your own and I'm going to say it.

Deirdre 1
Polly 2 } (*together*) Yes, Mother.
Jenny 3

Emma I'm very fond of you indeed, you know I am, but in some ways you've been more worry to us than both your sisters put together.

Polly 2 (*rising and going upstairs*) Mother, since I'm here I might as well make myself useful.

Jenny 3 starts to speak here

What about the beds? I'll see if I'm more successful with them than I am in the kitchen. I'll spend an eventful and meaningful morning folding sheets.

Jenny 3 (*rising and starting to speak during Polly 2's speech*) I think I'll just finish off in the kitchen, Mother.

Deirdre 1 starts to speak here

Get a little clearer. Then I can do the washing up. I thought we might sort out all that old china, too.

Deirdre 1 (*rising and speaking during Jenny 3's speech*) Excuse me, Ma. I'll just get the rest of my cases. Ollie's dumped them right down the bottom of the drive.

Polly 2 exits upstairs, Jenny 3 exits to the kitchen, Deirdre 1 goes out of the front door, all more or less simultaneously

Emma (*calling after them as they go, but in no particular direction*) Yes, you do that, dear. That's a good idea. (*She sighs and sits back*) Nice having her here for a little.

Edward (*laying down the remaining section of his paper*) Well, there's nothing worth reading in that. Well. Now that I've abandoned any hope of breakfast, I might as well work up an appetite for lunch. I think I'll go for another walk. How about you? You fancy a walk?

Emma Me? Oh. Well, it's a lovely morning.

Edward (*rising and crossing to the hall*) Come on then. I'll get my stick.

Emma Where were you planning on going?

Edward Oh, I don't know. My usual one. Cut across the fields at the back. Just as far as the chalk quarry. Walk back alongside the reservoir.

Emma Over the railway bridge and past the old sawmill? That way.

Edward If you like.

Emma Oh, yes. That's a lovely walk. Let's do that.

They move to the garden door

Do you think they'll be all right?

Edward Who?

Emma The children, dear.

Edward Possibly.

Emma If they can just keep working at their marriages. I'm sure that's the secret.

Edward Disastrous.

Emma That's the one thing you can say about us, Edward. We've never given up.

Edward Never for a minute.

Emma (*with just the slightest suspicion of a glint in her eye*) Here we go, then.

Edward (*staring at her, likewise*) Here we go...

They start to leave

Emma (*laughing*) Isn't this fun...!

Edward and Emma go out into the garden. As they go, Polly 2 comes out of the bedroom holding sheets and pillowcases. She doesn't see them

Polly 2 Mother, where do you want the... (*She sees no-one's there*) Mother? (*She goes to the stairs*)

Jenny 3 enters from the kitchen taking off washing-up gloves

Jenny 3 Mother, I'm going to put all the old dinner set in the... (*She sees no-one's there*) Mother? (*She stands listening*)

Deirdre 1 enters with more luggage through the front door

Deirdre 1 (*out of breath*) It's typical of Ollie to go and dump it all... (*She sees no-one's there*) Mother? (*She stands and listens*)

The following is spoken simultaneously

Polly 2 (*moving slowly to the front door; calling*) Mother... Father... Mother... Father... Where are you?

Jenny 3 (*moving slowly to the foot of the stairs and up them; calling*) Father... Mother... What are you doing...? Mother... (*She goes towards the bedroom*)

Deirdre 1 (*moving slowly towards the kitchen; calling*) Mother... Father... Where've you got to...? Mother...

Their calls continue, rising in tone with increasing alarm as they go off through their various exits and——

Black-out

FURNITURE AND PROPERTY LIST

Further dressing may be added at the director's discretion

ACT I

Scene 1

On stage: Tea table
Settee
Armchair
Chest of drawers containing coloured tins
Newspaper
Tea things
Bag containing knitting

Off stage: Table-cloth (**Emma**)
Stout stick (**Edward**)
2 plates of sandwiches (**Jenny**)
Luggage (**James**)
Plates of food (**Jenny**)
Plates (**Emma**)
Glass of water (**Jenny**)
Teapot (**Emma**)
Large bunch of flowers (**James**)
Handbag containing letter (**Polly**)
Flowers (**Edward**)

Personal: **Edward:** hat
David: bottle of pills

Scene 2

On stage: As before

Off stage: Flowers (**Edward**)
Flowers in plain vase (**Deirdre**)

Sandwiches on plate (**Emma**)
Pills (**Jenny**)
Glass of water, pills (**David**)

ACT II

SCENE 1

On stage: As before

Off stage: Handbag (**Polly**)
Trayful of cups (**Deirdre**)
David's coat (**Deirdre**)
Mug of milk, tin of biscuits (**Emma**)
Hacksaw (**Edward**)
Flannel (**Emma**)

SCENE 2

On stage: As before

Off stage: Breakfast things (**Emma**)
Suitcases (**James**)
Suitcase (**Polly**)
Cloth (**David**)
Handbag (**James**)
Fruit juice, bags of eggs (**Emma**)
Coffee, bowl of cereal (**Polly**)
James's suitcase (**Jenny**)
Breakfast tray. *On it:* two pieces of toast, small pot of coffee, etc.
     (**James**)
Plate of porridge (**Jenny**)
Fruit juice (**Polly**)
Glass of water (**Jenny**)
Bag (**James**)
Pair of old, rolled up trousers (**Oliver**)
Toast (**Polly**)
2 suitcases (**Deirdre**)
Sheets and pillowcases (**Polly**)
Luggage (**Deirdre**)

LIGHTING PLOT

Property fittings required: nil
1 Interior. The same throughout

ACT I, Scene 1

To open: Overall general lighting

Cue 1   **Edward** looks round threateningly   (Page 22)
             Black-out

ACT I, Scene 2

To open: Overall general lighting

Cue 2   **James** is left standing bewildered   (Page 39)
             Black-out

ACT II, Scene 1

To open: General evening lighting

Cue 3   **James** collapses   (Page 51)
             Black-out

ACT II, Scene 2

To open: General morning lighting

Cue 4   **All** exit, calling   (Page 79)
             Black-out

EFFECTS PLOT

ACT I

No cues

ACT II

Cue 1   **Emma**: "…been doing some woodwork?"   (Page 48)
         Tremendous crash off